⇥ DIY ⇤
CIRCUS LAB
for kids

DIY CIRCUS LAB

for kids

A Family-Friendly Guide for Juggling, Balancing, Clowning, and Show-Making

JACKIE LEIGH DAVIS

QUARRY

Brimming with creative inspiration, how-to projects, and useful information to enrich your everyday life, Quarto Knows is a favorite destination for those pursuing their interests and passions. Visit our site and dig deeper with our books into your area of interest: Quarto Creates, Quarto Cooks, Quarto Homes, Quarto Lives, Quarto Drives, Quarto Explores, Quarto Gifts, or Quarto Kids.

First Published in 2018 by Quarry Books, an imprint of The Quarto Group,
100 Cummings Center, Suite 265-D, Beverly, MA 01915, USA.
T (978) 282-9590 F (978) 283-2742 QuartoKnows.com

Quarry Books titles are also available at discount for retail, wholesale, promotional, and bulk purchase. For details, contact the Special Sales Manager by email at specialsales@quarto.com or by mail at The Quarto Group, Attn: Special Sales Manager, 401 Second Avenue North, Suite 310, Minneapolis, MN 55401, USA.

10 9 8 7 6 5 4 3 2

ISBN: 978-1-63159-347-5

Digital edition published in 2018

Library of Congress Cataloging-in-Publication Data available.

Design and page layout: Allison Meierding
Photography: Scot Langdon, Longhillphoto.com; except where indicated; also, Wikimedia Commons, pages 20, 46, 60, 84; Shutterstock.com, page 137.
Illustrations: Sara Morgan Greene, pages 68, 69, 76, 77.

Printed in China

For Rick

November 10, 1950–September 7, 2015

Teaching circus was Rick's cause and passion. For twelve years he traveled to elementary schools throughout New England as a Circus Smirkus artist-in-residence and school residency director. He believed that Smirkus residencies "allow students to discover they're capable of feats they never knew they could do."

Rick Davis. Credit: Peg Davis.

Rick originated CircusSecrets to help students attain their circus goals, but he also felt they could be used as "a tool kit for life" to achieve success in anything. Serving as a founding member of the American Youth Circus Organization was among his most important accomplishments.

Rick had been a clown with Ringling Brothers Barnum & Bailey Circus. Supported by the Peace Corps, he traveled to fifteen developing countries "in search of the comic denominator," offering free clown shows in villages, orphanages, and refugee camps.

Rick also performed at the 1982 World's Fair (where he met his wife, Jackie), Radio City Music Hall, the White House, and Walt Disney's Epcot Center. He was known as the Professor of Totally Useless Skills, teaching fun tricks and stunts that were the subjects of two books, *Totally Useless Skills* and *Totally Useless Office Skills*.

It was on Rick's to-do list to write another book . . . about teaching circus arts to kids.

Rick and Jackie. Credit: Courtesy of the author.

CONTENTS

PREFACE

Hey there, Reader!

Don't skip ahead just yet! Let me take a look at you . . .

Yup, you're just the person this book is for. You are entirely perfect for learning circus!

If you're heavily built, or thin, or in between—if you're tall, short, or middlin'—
Circus is for you.
  If you have a physical disability, or you don't—
If you're athletic, or you're not, or you're sort of—
Circus is for you. Because circus is for everybody.

If your skin is dark, or light, a mix of both, or any beautiful shade—
Circus is for you. Because circus sees all colors.

If you're flunking out of school, if you're honors or AP,
If you're somewhere in between—
If you have a learning disability, or you don't—
Circus is for you. Because circus knows you're more than test scores.

If you're super popular, or spend time alone, or people think you're weird—
Circus is for you. Because circus is inclusive. Circus is for everyone.

You are capable of doing things that you never thought you could do before. You can go as far as your willpower, and your interest, and your motivation will take you.

Let's do some circus!

Circusfully,

Jackie *(the author)*

CircEsteem, Chicago, IL. Credit: Lucy Little.

A LITTLE STORY

Years ago, my friend Rob Mermin was a mime and clown performing in small circuses across Europe. As he traveled with the circus families, he noticed how cool the circus kids were. They were different from the "ordinary" kids he knew—circus kids were unusually hardworking and self-reliant. Rob got the idea that, somehow, growing up in the world of circus gave those kids "an education in life that was missing from normal schooling."

Rob believed this special circus education should be available to *all* kids. So in 1987, he decided to start his own youth circus in Vermont. True story: When he told his mom he wanted to start a circus, his mother said, "Circus shmirkus, go get a real job!" And that's what he named it: Circus Smirkus. Kids have been getting an education in life there ever since!

Circus Smirkus is one of many youth circus programs around the world making it possible for kids like you to learn circus. In the meantime, you can try some circus right here, right now. There's a lot you can do to get started on your own—that's what this book is for. Who knows? Maybe you'll get inspired to start your own circus like Rob Mermin did!

Opposite: Early Smirkus, 1988.
Credit: Circus Smirkus.

Rob Mermin. Credit: Melissa Mermin.

THE CIRCUS SKILLS

There are several families of circus skills, each with its own movement language. In the circus world, there are many more than what's listed here, but this is a good start. You can learn to "speak" any of the skills here, and the more skills you learn, the more fluent you'll be in the language of circus. You can become circus literate!

Skills in **bold** are taught in this book, enough to get started.

ACROBATICS, ACROBALANCE, AND PYRAMIDS

Acrobatics involve rolling, inverting, and jumping (cartwheels, handstands, handsprings, and tucks). **Acrobalance** involves two acrobats sharing their centers of gravity as they support and balance each other (partner acrobatics, hand-to-hand). **Human pyramids** involve a group of people climbing upon and supporting each other in posed formations.

Flying Gravity Circus, Wilton, NH. Credit: Saibhung Singh Kalsa.

Sadly, we could not include any aerial skills in this book. They are not DIY skills but require a real, live teacher and a certified rigger to safely hang the equipment from a structurally sound ceiling (*never* a tree!). Please check out Appendix C at the back of the book to look for an aerial arts teacher near you.

AERIAL ARTS

Aerial arts are performed in the air and include trapeze, corde lisse, cloud swing, silks, straps, Spanish web, and lyra.

BALANCE ARTS

Equilibristics include unicycle, **tightrope** or tightwire, slackwire, rolling globe, **rola bola**, ladders, chair balancing, and **stilts**. Headstands, handstands, and standing on shoulders are balance skills, too.

My Nose Turns Red, Cincinnati, OH. Credit: Matt Steffen.

The Circus Project, Portland, OR. Credit: Isometric Studios.

CLOWNING

The **clown** is an eccentric, exquisitely imperfect human, in contrast to the mythical, superhuman circus artist. Using slapstick, mime, dance, and physical comedy, clowns elicit laughter through their comical struggles and peculiar perspectives.

Trenton Circus Squad, Trenton, NJ. Credit: Isometric Studios.

Diabolist Copper Santiago. Credit: Jim Cole.

Amazing Grace Circus, Nyack, NY. Credit: Deborah Grosmark Photography.

GYROSCOPIC JUGGLING

Gyroscopic juggling includes objects that you *spin*—such as **diabolos**, **juggling sticks** (flower or devil sticks), plates, batons, clubs, and staffs—as well as foot juggling and trick roping. Also spun are flow props (such as **poi** and **hoops**) and fire sticks. Juggling routines with these props often include dance and creative bodywork.

TOSS JUGGLING

Toss juggling involves objects that you *throw*, like **scarves**, **balls**, rings, clubs, and torches. Juggling and spinning are types of "object manipulation," which includes contact juggling, feather balancing, **hat tricks**, and lots more.

WHAT'S IN THIS BOOK?

This book empowers you to take your first steps in circus.

Unit introductions: Each unit begins with some background information about the skills, some interesting "circademic" factoids connecting circus to science, and a couple of CircusSecrets—simple but powerful tips for learning circus (and just about anything else).

Make your own props: This book teaches only skills using props you can make yourself (some props require power tools, so be sure to get adult help for those). These homemade props work well for starting out, and cost much less money. If you'd rather buy your props, we provide some suggestions at the end of the book.

>> Look for the link to our online prop-making tutorial videos!

Teach yourself some circus basics: The skills in this book can be safely learned within a few minutes up to a few weeks, depending on the skill and the effort you put in. These circus lessons teach you only *the very first steps*, the ABCs, in each skill. ABC stands for *Achievable Basic Competency*—the bare bones needed before you move on to more challenging tricks in that skill. When you pass the Level 1 Mastery Tests in each unit, use the resources at the end of the book to take your next steps.

>> Look for the link to our online skills tutorial videos!

Making a Show: This unit shows you and your friends how to link tricks together into an act, and link acts together into a whole show. We offer a toolbox with tips for working together in a positive, constructive way.

Growing Circus in Your Community: After you learn some skills, then what? Learning circus skills is just the beginning. We share ideas so you can keep doing, and sharing, circus.

For teachers, parents, and young readers: Appendix A lists ideas for using Circus as a Serious Tool for Learning, and it tells you how the CircusSecrets Are Linked to Social and Emotional Learning. Appendix B explains the Origins of Youth Circus and introduces the important work of Social Circus. Appendix C maps all the current youth circus programs in the United States and provides a snapshot of youth circus activity worldwide. The Resources provide suggestions for shopping, further study, and next steps in your circus learning.

Finally, you can learn about the Circus Lab kids who modeled for this book; the team that made this book possible, including Circus Smirkus (Vermont's award-winning youth circus); and me, the author.

So hey! Let's do some circus!

DISCLAIMER:
PROCEED AT YOUR OWN RISK! ⓘ

To the Reader:

Learning any circus skill involves the chance that you could get hurt. There is no such thing as zero risk. But *circus teaches you how to manage risk*—how to work smart and practice safely.

When making the props in this book, the (!) icon means you should take extra care with sharp tools.

When trying the skills in this book or our online tutorials, *practice safely*, especially with the partner acro, pyramids, and balance skills. If we recommend a spotter, don't do it without one. **Get help!**

Not all circus skills are do-it-yourself. The skills in this book are introductory activities in which the inherent risks are minimal and reasonably managed. They're meant to spark interest in circus arts so the young reader will be inspired to seek out a circus program with real live teachers. Please don't pursue higher level circus skills by yourself.

I, the author, and Quarry Books, the publisher, will not be responsible should you injure yourself in any way while doing any activity in this book or on the video tutorials. By purchasing or using this book and online tutorials, you agree to this disclaimer.

Be Smart, Practice Safely!

UNIT 1

SPINNING
and
FLOWING

Welcome to spinning and flowing!

This unit includes two kinds of twirling props you can make yourself. "Spinning" (or "gyroscopic juggling" to be exact) includes juggling sticks and diabolo. These are spun but also thrown and caught, so they're like toss juggling, too. "Flowing" includes poi and hoop. These mostly stay in contact with your hands or body and swoop around you in awesome patterns.

Once you get basic control of these props, you can begin to play, explore, and "flow" in new ways.

Opposite: Circus Harmony Diabolo Dudes, St. Louis, MO. Credit: Patti Chambers.

Introduction: ABOUT SPINNING AND FLOWING, CIRCADEMICS, AND CIRCUSSECRETS

Devil sticks.

Bamboo Chinese yo-yo.

Girl hula hooping, 1958.

Traditional Maori poi.
Credit: Polynesian Cultural Center.

"Stick play" probably originated in China during the Han Dynasty (206 BCE–220 CE). It involves spinning a wooden dowel, or baton, with two handsticks, and it's devilishly difficult because the baton moves so quickly. To slow it down, tassels or "flowers" were added (in the 1970s), and the flower stick, a.k.a. juggling stick, was born.

The Chinese yo-yo (*kōngzhú*) is made from two discs connected by an axle, spun on a string between two handsticks. Traditionally they're made of bamboo, and they whistle when spun. In 1906 a Belgian engineer, Gustave Philippart, patented the modern diabolo, which became a popular obsession in France and England. "Diabolo" comes from the Greek *dia bolo*, which means "across throwing." It's still popular today!

Hula hooping was a huge fad in the 1950s, but humans have played with hoops for thousands of years—from ancient Egypt and ancient Greece to medieval Europe and colonial America. Among the indigenous peoples of the Americas, the Hoop Dance is considered a sacred healing art. Modern "hooping" jumped in popularity in the 1990s and is performed for fun, fitness, and artistic expression.

Chinese "meteors" have cousins called *poi* that originate from the Maori people of New Zealand. *Poi* means "ball on a cord." The Maori swing poi in martial arts, games, and in women's dance performances. Modern poi are spun around the world at Flow Arts festivals.

CIRCUSSECRETS:
Pause, Imagine

Did you know your mood can affect how well you learn—for better or for worse? If you were just teased in the cafeteria, you might be in a lousy mood and it feels like the diabolo is not cooperating. But, if you just got an A on a test, you might feel great, ready to show that diabolo who's boss.

So before you start your circus practice, use the CircusSecret **pause** to *notice* what you're feeling in that moment. Take a few breaths. Check in with yourself and ask what's going on.

Then use the CircusSecret **imagine** to remember that you can learn anything you set your mind to through dedication and hard work. So imagine yourself doing the skill successfully and you will make it happen!

Use these CircusSecrets whenever you do circus—or when you do anything at all.

CIRCADEMICS:
Putting a Spin on It

Let's geek out on the physics of gyroscopic juggling. In "concentric" spinning, an object spins around its geometric center. A diabolo's axis is in the center, and so is a juggling stick's, at the middle of the baton.

Poi spin concentrically, with your hand at the center of rotation and the poi head tracing a circle.

When hooping, your body is the center of rotation (the axis), but the hoop spins around its edge. This is "eccentric" spinning, where the axis is not in the center. To keep the hoop spinning, you apply "centripetal force" *toward* the center of rotation while the hoop itself pushes *away* from the center in equal measure using "centrifugal force."

Here's a circus factoid: The size of a circus ring is 42 feet (12.7 m). This was determined by trick riders as the optimal circumference for standing on the backs of horses as they galloped around the ring. Dr. Quark, who teaches slapstick science (www.slapstickscience. com), says, "If the ring is smaller, the horses exert too much centripetal force (or the acrobats exert too much centrifugal force) and the rider goes toppling over the ring curb into the audience. If the ring is bigger, the acrobats just fall back off again because there isn't enough centrifugal force to keep them on the horse."

JUGGLING STICKS

Homemade juggling sticks work really well and cost less than commercial ones. Our plan includes two hex nuts on each end, but you can experiment with three and see if you prefer the extra weight. Some plans use strips of rubber inner tube, which has good grippiness and weight, but we like shelf liner for more color options.

NOTE: Here's the link to our companion online tutorial for making juggling sticks: www.DIYCircusLab.com/tutorials.

MAKE A SET OF JUGGLING STICKS

1. Measure the dowels, put on the safety glasses, and cut the dowels with a saw so you have: (!)

   a. one length at 22" (56 cm) (for the *baton*)
   b. two lengths, each 18" (45 cm) (for the *control sticks*)

THE BATON

1. On the 22" (56 cm) rod (baton), twist two hex nuts onto each end of the dowel *(Fig. 1)*. If the nuts are loose, use duct tape to anchor them to the dowel.

Fig. 1 Add two hex nuts on each end of the baton.

TIME NEEDED

About 1 hour

MATERIALS

* ruler or tape measure
* 2 hardwood dowels, ½" x 36" (1.3 x 91 cm)
* safety glasses
* saw (!)

* 4 standard hex nuts, ½" (1.3 cm)
* duct tape (any color)
* scissors
* at least 1 roll anti-skid shelf liner (or 2 rolls in contrasting colors)
* 1 roll colored electrician's tape

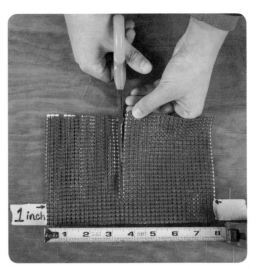

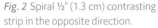

Fig. 2 Spiral ½" (1.3 cm) contrasting strip in the opposite direction.

Fig. 3 Cut fringe "flowers."

Fig. 4 Wrap and tape fringe on the ends.

2. Cut the shelf liner 1" (2.5 cm) wide along the entire length of the roll.

3. Duct tape the 1" (2.5 cm) strip to the baton just behind the hex nuts. Spiral the strip tightly to cover the entire baton, overlapping the edges. Tape the other end.

4. Cut a ½" (1.3 cm) strip of contrasting shelf liner and spiral it in the opposite direction down the baton, taping both ends *(Fig. 2)*.

5. For the fringe, cut two rectangles from the shelf liner measuring 8" x 5" (20 x 12.5 cm). Cut fringe in ½" (1.3 cm) strips, stopping 1" (2.5 cm) from the bottom *(Fig. 3)*. Optional: Use a contrasting color for the second rectangle.

6. Wrap the fringe around each end of the baton, taping securely just under the hex nuts *(Fig. 4)*. Wrap strips of colored electrician's tape at the middle and near the flowers at each end. Ta-da!

THE CONTROL STICKS

1. Just as you wrapped the baton, wrap each 18" (45 cm) stick with a 1" (2.5 cm)-wide shelf liner strip. Tape each end.

2. Add a contrasting strip (½" [1.3 cm] wide), spiraling in the opposite direction. Tape. Done!

JUGGLING STICKS

NOTE: Here's the link to our companion online tutorial for making juggling sticks: www.DIYCircusLab.com/tutorials.

STEP 1: HOLD THE STICKS

1. Grasp the sticks as shown *(Fig. 1)*.

2. Hold the sticks like railroad tracks on a tabletop—parallel to each other *and* to the floor. If the sticks droop down, the baton will roll off.

3. Practice the motion of the sticks: UP-DOWN, like drumming, bending at the elbow. Don't push them side to side.

STEP 2: SWEEP THE BATON

1. Sit cross-legged on the floor *(Fig. 2)*. Hold your sticks like railroad tracks. Lean the baton onto your right stick, with the bottom flower near your left knee.

2. With a quick motion, LIFT UP your right stick so the baton jumps over and lands on the left stick. The bottom flower should sweep over to your right knee *(Fig. 3)*. Do the same with the left stick: quickly LIFT UP to jump the baton back to the right stick. The bottom flower sweeps back to your left knee.

3. Repeat this many times rhythmically: tick, tock, tick, tock.

4. When you've got it going, LEAN BACK to lift the baton off the floor.

STEP 3: STANDING TICK-TOCK

1. Crouch down and set up the baton like in step 1 *(Fig. 4)*. Repeat the sweeping motion by LIFTING the sticks.

2. Continue the tick-tock motion and stand up, lifting the baton off the floor.

3. Keep the tick-tock going as long as you can. The goal is 20 tick-tocks.

Fig. 1 Hold the sticks like this.

Fig. 2 Sit cross-legged; the baton leans on the right stick.

Fig. 3 Lift the baton over to the left stick.

Fig. 4 Crouch in ready position.

STEP 4: THE FLIP, THE FINISH

Fig. 5 Flip the baton.

1. As you're doing the tick-tock, give your favorite stick an extra LIFT to flip the baton into the air *(Fig. 5)*. Catch and continue the tick-tock.

2. Try different flips: a half-flip, a full flip, or maybe a double or triple flip.

3. Practice flipping the baton from the right and from the left.

4. Flip and catch for a big finish.

STEP 5: TAKE THE LEVEL 1 MASTERY TEST

1. Twenty tick-tocks.

2. Flip one way.

3. Flip the other way.

4. Flip and catch, style and smile!

When you can do these ABCs on your own, you're ready for your Next Steps! See Resources on page 140.

TIPS

- Important: The bottom flower should sweep from one knee to the other. Don't plant the flower in the middle so only the top moves side to side.
- The sticks should connect with the baton on the tape near the flowers, not near the center.

DIABOLO

TIME NEEDED

About 1 hour

MATERIALS

Diabolo

* 2 heavyweight plastic dog bowls, crock style, 6" (15 cm) diameter ("medium")
* 2 lug nuts, acorn bulge, open-ended*
* 1 threaded rod, 4" (10 cm) long*
* 4 fender washers
* 2 rubber washers
* 2 hex nuts*

Important: The lug nuts, threaded rod, and hex nuts must all have the same *thread size* and *thread pitch*, whether standard (inches) or metric (millimeters). We found lug nuts that were 12 mm (size) x 1.75 (pitch), so we got a threaded rod and hex nuts to match; 12 mm x 1.50 hardware, or the standard equivalent, would also work. If you can't find a threaded rod, buy a 4" (10 cm) bolt and use a hacksaw to remove the head. (!)

Control Sticks

* 1 hardwood dowel, ½" x 36" (1.3 x 91 cm)
* 2–3 yards (2–3 m) synthetic string, braided not twisted ("mason's" or "construction line")

Tools

* utility knife (!)
* safety glasses
* power drill with an ⅛" (3 mm) bit and a bit the same diameter as the threaded rod (!)
* scrap wood block for drilling
* 2 adjustable/crescent wrenches
* tape measure
* pencil
* handsaw (!)
* scissors
* lighter (!)

We thought making a diabolo would be impossible!

You should have seen us trying to figure this out—we tried plungers (nope) and CDs sandwiched with foam on a lathed wooden rod (nope). Then our Makerspace geek, Joe Gaudreau, brilliantly thought of using lug nuts for the axle—and *voilà*! For the basic tricks, it really works!!

NOTE: Here's the link to our companion online tutorial for making a diabolo: www.DIYCircusLab.com/tutorials.

MAKE THE DIABOLO

1. Using a utility knife, carefully remove the small bump on the bottom of each bowl, creating a dimple for the drill. (!)

2. Put on the safety glasses. Using your larger bit, and placing a block of wood under the bowl, *slowly and carefully* drill a hole in each bowl *(Fig. 1)*. If you drill too fast, or push too hard, the bowl will crack. (!)

3. Screw the two lug nuts onto the threaded rod so the tapered ends face each other at dead center. Test for balance by hanging the axle on a string *(Fig. 2)*, then tighten using two wrenches. Re-check balance on string.

4. Assemble from the centered lug nuts outward to the ends of the threaded rod in this order *(Fig. 3)*: fender washer, bowl, rubber washer, fender washer, hex nut. Tighten.

5. Done!

MAKE THE HANDSTICKS

1. Measure the dowel and use a pencil to mark it into two lengths of 16" (40.5 cm). Cut the dowel with a saw. (!)

2. With the ⅛" (3 mm) bit, drill a hole that is ½" (1.3 cm) from one end of each stick *(Fig. 4)*. (!)

3. Measure string from the floor to your collarbone, adding 3" (7.5 cm). Cut and cauterize the end of the string with a lighter. (!)

4. Thread the string through the hole *(Fig. 5)*. Tie a monster knot. Repeat on the other stick. (Experienced diabolists tie a *follow-through figure-8 knot*—ask a Boy Scout.) Done!

Fig. 1 Carefully drill a hole in the bowl.

Fig. 2 Test for balance on a string.

Fig. 3 Assemble in this sequence.

Fig. 4 Drill a hole in one end of each stick.

Fig. 5 Thread the string through the handsticks.

DIABOLO

> ## ! SAFETY FIRST!
> When you pop the diabolo up, it could come down and hit you or someone else. Always check your surroundings before you pop it, and if it looks like it's headed toward someone's head, shout the warning "HEADS!" Practice smart, practice safely!

NOTE: Here's the link to our companion online tutorial on diabolo ABCs: www.DIYCircusLab.com/tutorials.

STEP 1: THE ROLLING START

In these directions, the diabolo is controlled by the right hand, so we call the right stick the control stick. If you're a lefty, your control stick will be the left one. Switch all "rights" to "lefts" below.

1. Hold the handsticks like railroad tracks on a table-top—parallel to each other *and* to the floor. Place the diabolo on the string, on the floor, on your right *(Fig. 1)*.

2. Step sideways to your left and roll the diabolo from right to left. Gently LIFT it and immediately begin tug-tug-tugging your right stick *(Figs. 2 and 3)*. Tugging is like drumming lightly. This motion pulls the diabolo into a spin. Keep the left hand STILL.

Fig. 1 Ready position.

3. Repeat: STEP, ROLL, LIFT, TUG. The faster it spins, the more stable it will be for tricks.

Fig. 2 Step and roll.

Fig. 3 Lift and tug.

Fig. 4 Near bowl down? Push the right stick forward.

Fig. 5 Near bowl up? Pull the right stick back.

STEP 2: CORRECTING THE TILT

As you spin, the diabolo will tilt away or toward you. Keep an eye on the bowl closest to you—the "near" bowl:

1. If the near bowl starts tilting *down*, push your control stick (right) *forward* (away from you) as you tug-tug-tug (*Fig. 4*). The string pushes against the far bowl, which tips the near bowl back up.

2. If the near bowl starts tilting *up*, pull your control stick (right) *back* (toward you) as you tug-tug-tug (*Fig. 5*). The string pulls on the near bowl, which tips it back down.

3. Keep your knees pointing toward the near bowl. If the near bowl starts rotating sideways, shift your feet so your knees point toward the bowl again. Check that the ends of your handsticks are even—if one is ahead of the other, you're rotating the diabolo yourself.

STEP 3: THE POP-UP

Learn the pop-up only when you can spin fast and control the tilt. You need a high ceiling for this! Or go outside.

1. *Without* the diabolo, practice the SNAP, POINT, CATCH:

    a. SNAP your sticks apart so the string is *tight*. This movement pops the diabolo straight up.

    b. POINT the control stick to the sky. Eyeball the imaginary diabolo in the air.

    c. CATCH the imaginary diabolo on the string.

Make sure these are three separate movements: snap, THEN point, THEN catch. If you snap and point in one move, your diabolo will fling sideways.

2. *With* the diabolo, get it spinning wicked fast. Do the SNAP to pop it *(Fig. 6)*, POINT your stick *(Fig. 7)*, and CATCH *(Fig. 8)*.

3. Repeat a lot! The goal is three times in a row with no drops.

Fig. 6 SNAP…

Fig. 7 … POINT …

Fig. 8 … and CATCH.

STEP 4: POP AND STOP

1. To stop the diabolo, pop it as in step 3.

2. Quickly shift the sticks into your less-favorite hand so you can...

3. ...CATCH the diabolo in your favorite hand, squeezing the axle tight *(Fig. 9)*.

CAUTION: Use "soft hands" when you catch, continuing the downward motion with your arm to absorb the impact. Squeeze tight to stop the spin so you don't get a friction burn.

STEP 5: TAKE THE LEVEL 1 MASTERY TEST

1. Rolling start.

2. Correct the tilt—to front and back.

3. Pop and catch three times.

4. Pop and stop. Style and smile!

When you can do these ABCs on your own, you're ready for your Next Steps! See Resources on page 140.

Fig. 9 Put both sticks into one hand, catch, and choke the diabolo.

HOOP

TIME NEEDED

1 hour

MATERIALS

* black irrigation tubing, ¾" (18 mm) diameter polyethylene, 100 psi
* PVC cutters (ratchet cutting action is best) ⚠
* pot of boiling water ⚠
* tubing connector (called an HDPE connector), ¾" (18 mm)
* at least 2 rolls colored duct tape or other decorative tape

NOTE: For smaller children, a lighter weight hoop might be best. In this case, use ½" (13 mm) tubing and ½" (13 mm) tubing connector. The tubing comes in 100' (30 m) rolls, and you need a special cutter, plus the tape.

It's great to make a hoop that fits your height exactly. And homemade hoops are heavier, so they spin more slowly for better learning. The expense of materials can add up, though, so consider sharing the cost with your hooping friends. Throw a hoop-making party!

NOTE: Here's the link to our companion online tutorial for making a hoop: www.DIYCircusLab.com/tutorials.

MAKE A HOOP

1. While standing, measure a loop of tubing to the height of your bellybutton *(Fig. 1)*.

2. Carefully cut the tubing with the PVC cutters *(Fig. 2)*. (!)

3. Dip the ends of the tubing into boiling water for at least 20 seconds *(Fig. 3)*. (!)

4. Insert the tubing connector into one end and press the other end over it until the ends of the tube meet *(Fig. 4)*.

5. Join the ends with duct tape.

6. Take a roll of colored duct tape and make a split in the end. Carefully lay down a spiral of tape all around the hoop.

7. Do the same, but in the opposite direction, with a second color of tape *(Fig. 5)*. Done!

Fig. 1 Measure a circle of tubing at your belly button.

Fig. 2 Cut the tubing with PVC cutters.

Fig. 3 Put the ends of the tubing in boiling water.

Fig. 4 Insert tube connector and connect both ends.

Fig. 5 Apply a second spiral of tape in the opposite direction.

HOOPING

STEP 1: FRONT HAND SPIN
(AKA VERTICAL LASSO)

This series of moves shows "off-body" tricks.

1. Hold the hoop in the *front plane*, grasping it at the bottom with your palm down *(Fig. 1)*.

2. Let the hoop fall to one side and spin it around the hand. Pulse the hand up and down, with your thumb up and your elbow next to your body *(Fig. 2)*.

3. To switch hands, keep spinning as you slip your second hand next to the first, pressing both palms together *(Fig. 3)*. Slip the first hand out and continue spinning on the second hand.

Fig. 1 Hold the hoop at the bottom.

Fig. 2 Spin the hoop in the front plane, with your hand open, thumb up.

NOTE: Here's the link to our companion online tutorial on hooping ABCs: www.DIYCircusLab.com/tutorials.

4. Practice switching and controlling the hoop on your hands.

STEP 2: BREAKS (REVERSE DIRECTIONS)

1. Continue the front spin that you just learned.

2. As the hoop comes around, grab and squeeze it to stop the motion, then send it in the reverse direction.

3. Practice breaks in the front plane in both directions (left and right) with each hand.

STEP 3: SIDE SPIN (ANOTHER FORM OF VERTICAL LASSO)

1. Start with the front spin (see STEP 1).

2. While spinning, turn your body a quarter turn so that the hoop is at your side in the *side plane (Fig. 4)*. Your fingers point out to the side, with your palm forward, thumb up.

3. Stop the hoop, then spin it in the opposite direction.

4. Turn a quarter turn back to the front. Press your palms together, switch hands, and turn a quarter turn the other way.

5. Practice breaks in the side plane, facing both directions, switching between forward and backward spins. This movement flows naturally into the forward weave.

Fig. 3 Place your palms together to switch hands.

Fig. 4 Turn to spin in the side plane.

STEP 4: FORWARD WEAVE

In this trick, the hoop swings across your body and back again in a figure eight. It's the same movement as crossing forward with poi (see next section). You can try the movement without the hoop first.

1. Start with the hoop hanging at your side, with your palm up and your thumb facing behind you *(Fig. 5)*.

2. Leading with your thumb:
   - raise the hoop up behind you, thumb up *(Fig. 6)*
   - turn your thumb down and swoop down across your body *(Fig. 7)*
   - continue up behind you, turning your thumb up *(Fig. 8)*
   - follow your thumb back to the first side *(Fig. 9)*.

3. Repeat with a fluid motion. Loosen your grip so the hoop can play freely. A tight grip makes the weave harder.

4. Try connecting the side spin with the forward weave.

Fig. 5 Weave starting position.

Fig. 6 Raise the hoop up behind you.

Fig. 7 Weave across your body, thumb down.

Fig. 8 Turn your thumb up to come back.

STEP 5: WAIST HOOPING

This is the classic "on-body" hoop movement. It helps to wear close-fitting clothes.

1. Stand with one foot forward. Hold the hoop around your body.

2. Wind up for a big flat spin and push the hoop into action.

3. Pulse *back and forth* from your belly (not in a circle). *(Fig. 10)*
   - If the hoop drops, pulse faster.
   - Use your belly, not your legs too much.
   - Use your tall circus posture—don't bend forward or the hoop will drop.

When you can do these ABCs on your own, you're ready for your Next Steps! See Resources on page 140.

Fig. 9 Return to the first side.

Fig. 10 Use your belly!

POI

TIME NEEDED

10 minutes

MATERIALS

* 1 cup (160 g) rice (or dried lentils or beans)
* 2 plastic baggies
* 4 rubber bands
* pair of knee socks (stripes are fun!)

Making poi is quick, simple, and fun. We use rice here, but you can use dried lentils, popcorn, or whatever you have. Watch out if there are mice in your house—they'll eat your poi. You can also put an old tennis ball into a sock. This makes lighter poi but—sorry—they will still smack you!

NOTE: Here's the link to our companion online tutorial for making poi: www.DIYCircusLab.com/tutorials.

Fig. 1 Pour the rice into a baggy.

Fig. 2 Slip the bags into the socks and tie the ends.

MAKE A PAIR OF POI

1. Measure out ½ cup (80 g) of rice (lentils, beans) and pour it into a baggie.

2. Twist the baggie closed and tightly wrap it with two rubber bands.

3. Repeat with the second baggie *(Fig. 1)*.

4. Slip each baggie into the end of each sock *(Fig. 2)*.

5. Tie a knot near the top of each sock. Make sure each knot is the same distance from the end. Done!

POI

STEP 1: GETTING STARTED

HOLDING THE POI

1. Hold out your hand, palm up.

2. Slip the knot between your index and middle fingers with the poi hanging down *(Fig. 1)*.

RAILROAD TRACKS (A.K.A. THE WHEEL PLANE)

1. Imagine you're standing between two railroad tracks that run along both sides of your feet, out ahead of you (front) and out behind you (back).

Fig. 1 Hold the poi like this.

2. Spin the poi along the line of the tracks, creating circles next to your body like wheels on a big wheelchair.

STEP 2: ONE POI—FORWARD, BACKWARD, CROSSING

1. Starting with *one* poi in your favorite hand, stand facing front (looking down the tracks). Swing your arm back and forth along the railroad track to get a feel for the poi's weight.

NOTE: Here's the link to our companion online tutorial on poi ABCs: www.DIYCircusLab.com/tutorials.

2. Forward: Using just your forearm, swing the poi up behind you and *down the front* along the railroad track. Continue circling from the wrist *(Fig. 2)*.

    a. You know you're circling *Forward* if the poi hits your *Feet*.

    b. Switch hands and circle forward along the other track.

3. Backward: Using just your forearm, swing the poi up the front and *down behind you* along the railroad track. Continue circling from the wrist.

    a. You know you're circling *Backward* if the poi goes over your shoulder and hits your *Back*.

    b. Switch hands and circle backward along the other track.

4. Crossing Forward: This is the same motion as the forward weave in hooping.

    a. Circle one poi forward. As the poi swoops toward the back and UP, cross your arm over your body to the opposite side. Continue circling with your arm across your body *(Fig. 3)*.

    b. As the poi swoops back and UP, uncross your arm to the original side.

    c. Switch hands and repeat.

5. Crossing Backward:

    a. As the poi swoops toward the front and UP, cross your arm over your body to the opposite side. Keep circling along the opposite track.

    b. As the poi swoops forward and UP, uncross your arm to the original side.

    c. Switch hands and repeat.

Fig. 2 One poi forward.

Fig. 3 One poi across body (forward).

STEP 3: TWO POI—FORWARD AND BACK-WARD IN SAME-TIME AND SPLIT-TIME

Now pick up the second poi.

1. **Same-time:** Spin both poi forward along the railroad tracks together in the same rhythm. They are parallel to each other, as if connected by an invisible thread.

2. **Split-time:** Change the rhythm so the poi alternate, chasing each other: one-two, one-two, one-two *(Fig. 4)*.

3. Switch to spinning backward in same-time.

4. Spin backward in split-time.

STEP 4: THE TWO-BEAT WEAVE

1. FIRST: Spin both poi forward in *same-time*.

2. As the poi lift up behind you, cross your arms over your body and back again.

3. Repeat the same-time arm crossing, noticing which arm likes to go on top.

4. THEN: Spin forward in *split-time*.

5. Cross one arm over followed by the other, and back again *(Fig. 5)*. The second arm goes over the first arm.

Fig. 4 Two poi, split-time.

Fig. 5 Two-beat weave.

Fig. 6 Turning: Sweep poi toward floor as you pivot 180 degrees.

Fig. 7 Turning: Arc poi toward sky as you pivot back to where you started.

STEP 5: SAME-TIME TURNS WITH TWO POI

1. Spin both poi forward in *same-time*.

2. Extending your arms forward and DOWN, sweep both poi toward the floor as you pivot a half turn and face the opposite direction *(Fig. 6)*. You should now be spinning the poi backward.

3. From the backward spin, extend your arms forward and UP, arching both poi toward the ceiling as you pivot a half turn back to where you started *(Fig. 7)*. You're now spinning the poi forward again. (This makes much more sense in the video tutorial!)

STEP 6: TAKE THE LEVEL 1 MASTERY TEST WITH TWO POI

1. Forward and backward, same-time and split-time.

2. Two-beat weave.

3. Same-time turns.

4. Style and smile!

Once you can do these ABCs on your own, you're ready to take your Next Steps! See Resources on page 140.

UNIT 2

TOSS JUGGLING

Welcome to juggling!

Once you learn to juggle, fruit in the grocery store will never look the same . . .

In this unit, you can grab some plastic grocery bags and learn how to juggle "scarves" in one afternoon. Or make a set of juggling balls and try your hand at the world's most popular juggling pattern, the cascade. That will take longer than an afternoon for sure, so we've also thrown in Armpit Juggling, one of our favorite (and impressively silly) tricks.

Opposite: The Circus Lab Jugglers.

Jugglers painted in an Egyptian tomb.

Jugglers have been throwing and catching stuff throughout time. Some 4,000 years ago, hieroglyphs of female jugglers were etched in a tomb at Beni Hasan in Egypt. Over 2,000 years ago, a Greek artist from Attica painted a juggler girl on a wine-drinking cup. And in China, a warrior named Xiong Yiliao juggled nine balls in the middle of a battle, which frightened off 500 enemy soldiers and won the war! Now you can join the huge international family of jugglers.

Amazingly, some people wonder why they should bother to learn juggling. I hope this isn't you—but in case it is, here are five reasons to jump in:

1. Juggling is cool.

2. Juggling happens *everywhere*: in parades, festivals, talent shows, college clubs, TV, movies, summer camps, talk shows, TED Talks, hospitals, schools, parks, and, of course, circuses.

3. Juggling grows your brain! (See Circademics opposite.)

CIRCUSSECRETS:
Try, Try Again, Try a New Way

"I can't do that." Kids say this a lot when they see juggling. Well, Henry Ford said, "Whether you think you can, or you think you can't—you're right."

Learning to think *I can* begins with the Circus-Secret **try**.

And then: **try again**! And again, and again. Don't give up. Persistence, or *grit*, is just as important as talent for achieving success—whether it's juggling or anything else.

But—if Trying Again isn't working, **try a new way** coaches you to shift what you're doing—or how you're thinking—so you get closer to a breakthrough.

Don't quit. Take a break, but then come back. These CircusSecrets can help you motivate yourself to work toward, and achieve, your goals. Practice thinking *I can do it* until it becomes *I just did it!*

4. Juggling improves eye-hand coordination, peripheral vision, reaction time, and focus. Sport coaches recommend it for their players.

5. World Juggling Day happens every June. It was started by the awesome International Juggler's Association (www.juggle.org).

Every juggler—throughout time and around the world—started from zero. So if you're a brand-new beginner, you're in good company.

Let's juggle!

CIRCADEMICS:
Juggling and Your Brain

Neuroplasticity is the brain's ability to change in reaction to new situations. Did you know that part of your brain changes when you learn to juggle?

Scientist Dr. Draganski used magnetic resonance imaging (MRI) to look inside the living brains of people who were learning to juggle. He found that certain areas of their brains *grew* as they got better at it. Interestingly, those brain areas went back to normal size once the people stopped practicing, even though they could still juggle. So it's only when we're learning something new that parts of the brain grow.

Jugglers love to say that because "juggling grows your brain" it means juggling makes you smarter. Sadly, this probably isn't true. The brain areas that grow when you learn juggling (the visual cortex and intraparietal sulcus) are responsible for eye movements and eye-hand coordination, not for thinking. But learning to juggle makes you focus, set goals, and persist, which help you do well on your homework, and *that* makes you smarter. In any case, jugglers are already pretty smart—just ask one!

SCARF JUGGLING

Yes, it's true: even though they're an environmental menace, plastic grocery bags make excellent juggling props. We use biodegradable bags when possible.

> **NOTE:** Here's the link to our companion online tutorial on scarf juggling ABCs: www.DIYCircusLab.com/tutorials.

STEP 1: ONE SCARF

1. Make a duck hand. Hold one bag in the duck's mouth (*Fig. 1*).

2. Crossing your arm across your face, throw the bag to the opposite corner (*Fig. 2*).

3. With your other duck, snatch the bag out of the air and drop that arm down by your side (*Fig. 3*).

4. Now cross that arm across your face, throwing the bag back to the first duck's corner. Snatch it down with your first duck.

5. Play catch with your ducks! THROW ACROSS, SNATCH DOWN. Don't turn your ducks upside down—grab the bags fast and pull them down.

Fig. 1 One duck holding a bag.

Fig. 2 Duck throws the bag across your face.

Fig. 3 Snatch down with the other duck.

Fig. 4 Two ducks throw across...

Fig. 5 ...and snatch down.

Fig. 6 Hold two bags with one duck.

STEP 2: TWO SCARVES

1. Give a bag to each duck.

2. Throw each bag across your face—right THROW, left THROW (*Fig. 4*)—quickly uncross your arms, and snatch down—left CATCH, right CATCH (*Fig. 5*). Remember to throw UP ACROSS your body, and catch DOWN ALONGSIDE your body.

STEP 3: THREE SCARVES

1. Hold one bag in your right palm, leaving three fingers to make a baby duck (*Fig. 6*). Hold a second bag with the baby duck. Hold the third bag with your other duck.

2. Start with the hand that has two bags, THROW R (baby duck), THROW L, CATCH L, THROW R (bag in palm), CATCH R. Continue alternating R, L, R, L until you're juggling!

STEP 4: TAKE THE LEVEL 1 MASTERY TEST

1. Twenty throws and catches with a clean finish.

2. You did it!

JUGGLING BALLS

TIME NEEDED

About 30 minutes

MATERIALS

* sharp utility knife ⚠
* 3 old (or new) tennis balls
* funnel
* about 3 cups (500 g) of birdseed (enough to fill 3 tennis balls)
* about 1 yard (91 cm) of duct tape
* scissors
* 6 bright balloons, 12" (30 cm), in different colors

Filling tennis balls with birdseed makes them heavier for successful juggling.
It also makes them roll farther, so you'll get more exercise when you chase them around the room!

NOTE: Here's the link to our companion online tutorial for making juggling balls: www.DIYCircusLab.com/tutorials.

MAKE A JUGGLING BALL

1. With the utility knife, *carefully* cut a slit about 1½" (3.8 cm) long in one tennis ball. *It is difficult to puncture the tennis ball, so GET ADULT HELP (Fig. 1).* (!)

2. Squeeze the ball to open the "mouth." Insert the funnel.

3. Fill the ball with as much birdseed as you can jam in there *(Fig. 2).* (When you shake the ball, you shouldn't hear rattling.)

4. Tear off 10" (25 cm) of duct tape. Split that piece into three lengthwise strips.

5. Tightly wrap the first piece of tape over the opening and around the ball. Repeat with the second and third strips, overlapping the tape over the slit to seal it completely *(Fig. 3).*

6. With scissors, cut the entire mouth piece off two balloons.

7. Stretch one balloon all the way over the taped tennis ball. Stretch on the second balloon, making sure to cover the fuzzy belly button. Ta-da! One ball is done *(Fig. 4).*

8. Repeat steps 1–7 with the other two tennis balls. Ta-da! Three juggling balls!

Fig. 1 Cut the ball.

Fig. 2 Use the funnel to pour in birdseed.

Fig. 3 Wrap the ball with three strips of duct tape.

Fig. 4 Cover the ball.

THREE-BALL JUGGLING

NOTE: Here's the link to our companion online tutorial on three-ball juggling ABCs: www.DIYCircusLab.com/tutorials.

BEFORE YOU START

The basic three-ball pattern is called the *cascade*. The balls shoot up the middle and fall (cascade) down the sides. All three balls trace the same shape in the air: a sideways figure eight (infinity sign), with *two* peaks, one on either side of your head. The ball does *not* fly in an arc with *one* peak in the middle. This is a common mistake. Learning the figure eight of one ball will help you juggle all three. The motion is created by making circles with your lower arms. Practice this motion with the One-Ball Whoop-de-Doo game!

STEP 1: ONE-BALL "WHOOP-DE-DOO"

1. Start with ONE ball in the *ready position*, standing at relaxed attention, feet slightly apart, nose pointed slightly up (*Fig. 1*). Rest the ball in your favorite hand, palm up.

2. Using just your forearm, hold the ball and move it around in circles: UP THE MIDDLE, like zipping up a jacket.

Fig. 1 Ready position.

Fig. 2 One ball at zenith LEFT.

Fig. 3 One ball at zenith RIGHT.

3. Make three circles with the ball: one, two, three. On THREE, release the ball so it flies over to the other side *(Fig. 2)* and falls into your other upturned hand.

4. With that hand, make three circles up the middle—one, two, whoop-de-doo!—and release the ball back to your favorite hand *(Fig. 3)*.

TIPS

- Imagine a large picture frame in front of you. When you throw from your right, the ball peaks at the top left corner of the frame. When you throw from the left, the ball peaks at the top right corner.
- The ball should peak at the corners, never in the middle.
- Throw a little higher than your head.

5. Repeat "one, two, whoop-de-doo" about 20 times.

STEP 2: ONE-BALL "SCOOP-AND-FLY"

1. Continuing with one ball, throw the "whoop-de-doo" without the circles. Scoop the ball down and release it to the opposite corner. Catch and *immediately* scoop down and release to the other hand. Continue rhythmically about twenty times. See the figure eight?

TIPS

- Keep the ball in *perpetual motion*. Don't stop when you catch it. The moment of the catch *is precisely the same moment* of the next scoop.
- If the ball spins, you're flicking it off your fingers. Float the ball from your palm instead.

STEP 3: THROW 3, DROP 3

1. Now take *three* balls (yes three, not two). Hold two in your right hand, the third in your left, palms up *(Fig. 4)*.

2. Practice throwing Ball #1 while holding Ball #3.

Fig. 4 Balls #1 and #3 in right, #2 in left.

3. Stand in the *ready position*.

4. Starting right, circle and release one ball at a time—#1, #2, #3—but don't catch them, let them fall. Throw with circular, relaxed throws. THROW, THROW, THROW/PLOP, PLOP, PLOP *(Fig. 5)*.

5. Repeat with even, rhythmical plops.

TIPS

- Always start with the hand that has *two* balls.
- Throw each ball the SAME HEIGHT.
- *Listen* to each ball hitting the ground. The plops should be rhythmical and even.
- WAIT for all three balls to plop, THEN retrieve.

Fig. 5 THROW, THROW, THROW.

STEP 4: THROW 3, CATCH 1

1. Continue to THROW, THROW, THROW but CATCH *any one* of the balls and release it again *(Fig. 6)*. *Keep the arm circles going* even when balls drop.

2. Repeat a lot.

3. Continue to THROW, THROW, THROW but now CATCH *any two* balls and release them. Keep the arm circles going.

4. Repeat a lot.

Fig. 6 Throw two, catch one.

STEP 5: START JUGGLING!

1. Continue to THROW, THROW, THROW, but now CATCH *each ball* and throw it again. Continue the arm circles.

2. Count out loud every time a ball leaves your hand. Write down your daily record highest number of throws.

3. Practice a minimum of 10 minutes per day.

STEP 6: TAKE THE LEVEL 1 MASTERY TEST

1. Twenty-five throws and catches.

2. Clean finish.

Once you can do these ABCs on your own, you're ready to take your Next Steps! See Resources on page 140.

TIPS

- Practice over a couch or bed so when you drop the balls they are easier to pick up.
- If a ball jumps forward, or if two balls hit in the air, go back to one-ball whoop-de-doo to fix it.
- If things get wonky, take a break, or take a nap, or yodel. Your brain practices even when your body is resting.

ARMPIT JUGGLING

Fig. 1 Ready.

Fig. 2 Put Ball #1 in left armpit.

Three balls, two hands, two armpits. Let the fun begin! (Note that Ball #1 is yellow, Ball #2 is orange, and Ball #3 is red.)

1. Stand ready, two balls in the right hand, one ball in the left *(Fig. 1)*.

2. Right hand puts Ball #1 in left armpit *(Fig. 2)*.

3. Left hand puts Ball #2 in right armpit *(Fig. 3)*.

4. Notice your left hand is free. With both hands lowered, make a "basket" with your left hand, hooking it toward your thigh, opening the fingers wide *(Fig. 4)*.

5. Drop Ball #1 from your left armpit into your left hand *(Fig. 5)*. It works better if you don't look.

6. Notice your left armpit is now free. Right hand puts Ball #3 in left armpit *(Fig. 6)*.

7. What's free now? RIGHT! Make a basket with your right hand *(Fig. 7)*.

8. Drop Ball #2 from your right armpit into your right hand *(Fig. 8)*.

9. What's free now? You got it. Continue indefinitely. You could win a talent show with your armpits!

NOTE: Here's a link to our companion online tutorial on armpit juggling: www.DIYCircusLab.com/tutorials.

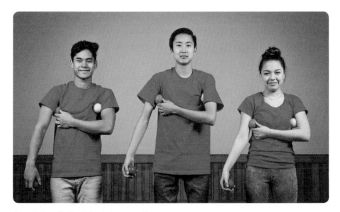

Fig. 3 Put Ball #2 in right armpit.

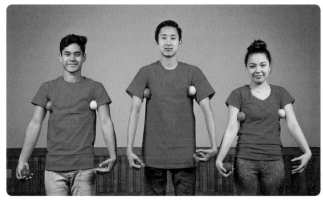

Fig. 4 Make a basket with left hand.

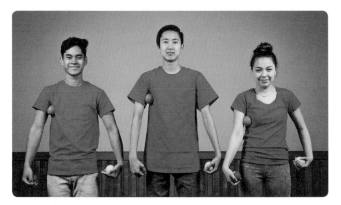

Fig. 5 Drop Ball #1 from left armpit into left basket.

Fig. 6 Put Ball #3 into left armpit.

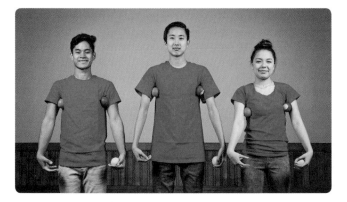

Fig. 7 Make a basket with right hand.

Fig. 8 Drop Ball #2 from right armpit into right basket.

BALANCE

Welcome to balance, or more circusfully, equilibristics!

You are hereby invited to stand or walk on top of unstable objects while smiling and making it look easy. Making these objects is easier than learning to use them—you'll need construction tools and an adult helper, but they don't take very long to build.

The rola bola, stilts, and tightrope will all improve your sense of balance. As you gain confidence, you might wonder what to do with your hands. It's a good reason to learn juggling, spinning, and flowing!

Opposite: The Prescott Circus Theatre, Oakland, CA. Credit: Gary G. Thomsen.

Introduction: ABOUT BALANCE, CIRCADEMICS, AND CIRCUSSECRETS

The Flying Wallendas.

The ancient Greeks had many words for tightrope walkers, but in 260 B.C.E. they were united under a single word: funambulus; from *funis* (a rope) and *ambulare* (to walk). Funambulists have astounded us through time: rope dancing for Napoleon Bonaparte; spanning wires across Niagara Falls, Notre Dame Cathedral, and the World Trade Towers; and setting Guinness World Records.

Stanley Washburn Jr., a World War II pilot, noticed African children balancing on a plank and log. He built his own version of this toy for his daughter, and in 1953 he patented the first Bongo Board. Circus folks modified his idea, stacking multiple cylinders, juggling while balancing, and standing on shoulders. By the 1960s, the "rolo bolo" was part of the circus industry.

CIRCUSSECRETS:
Go Slow, Step by Step

For most humans, circus learning takes time. The CircusSecret **go slow** reminds you that success begins at the beginning, not at the end. Circus doesn't reward you before you put in the work—but the work pays off if you take your time getting there. Little by little, you'll get better.

The CircusSecret **step by step** reminds you to build a solid foundation before moving on. In tight-rope walking, beginners often want to race across the rope before they lose their balance just to end up on the ground. Instead, walk slowly toe-to-toe, step and slide, finding your balance with each step. Going slow, step by step, is the faster way to mastery.

In China, stilt walking is a traditional folk art. Performances include a gentle, graceful style (*Wenqiao*) and a valiant, acrobatic style (*Wuqiao*). In the 1800s, shepherds in Landes, France, used "tchangues" (big legs) for navigating swampy terrain to keep watch over their sheep. In the Caribbean, brightly colored Moko Jumbies dance on stilts during Carnival. The Moko is a spirit figure brought over from Africa who protects people from evil. And now there's "powerbocking" on curved, spring-loaded stilts that let you jump like a kangaroo and run up to 20 miles per hour!

CIRCADEMICS:
Our Sixth Sense

Sight, hearing, smell, taste, touch. The ancient Greek philosopher Aristotle (384–322 B.C.E.) was the first person to classify the senses. Question: Which sense is the most important? Answer: Your sense of balance. Surprised?

Without balance, almost everything we do would be impossible. When something's wrong we feel dizzy, can't stand up, can't track words on a page, can't concentrate—and we feel really, really seasick. When everything's fine, we don't even notice it.

Good balance depends on:

- The vestibular system—structures in the inner ear that inform the brain about your head's position and movements
- The visual system—the eyes inform the brain about where you are and how you're moving in relationship to what's around you
- Proprioception—messages from the skin, muscles, and joints (especially in your neck and ankles) about the stretch and pressure within your body

Without balance, there wouldn't be circus! That's reason enough to convince Aristotle—if he were alive today—to add balance as the sixth sense.

ROLA BOLA

TIME NEEDED

20–30 minutes

MATERIALS

* tape measure
* 1" x 12" x 36"
  (2.5 x 30.5 x 91 cm) clear
  pine board (not plywood)
* pencil
* 2 sawhorses
* safety glasses (for
  power saw)
* crosscut or circular saw ⚠️

* wood glue
* power drill with T-20 bit ⚠️
* 4 self-drilling screws,
  1¼" (31 mm)
* latex paint and paintbrush
  (optional)
* 4 strips anti-skid tape
  (for board)
* 2 strips vinyl traction tape
  (for roller)
* PVC pipe, 4" diameter x 12½"
  (10 x 31.75 cm) (Ask to have
  it cut at the store.)

Use "self-drilling" screws rather than standard drywall screws. This will prevent the wood from splitting. You'll need to use a special T-20 bit.

NOTE: Here's the link to our companion online tutorial for making a rola bola: www.DIYCircusLab.com/tutorials.

MAKE A ROLA BOLA

1. Measure the board and mark a 32" (81.3 cm) length with pencil. Lay the wood across the sawhorses and cut at the marked line with the saw *(Fig. 1)*. (!)

2. From the remainder, measure and cut two 2" (5 cm) stops *(Fig. 2)*. (!)

3. Place the two stops at each end of the board, setting each one back 2" (5 cm) from the edge. Glue and screw them into place *(Fig. 3)*. (!)

Fig. 1 Saw the board.   *Fig. 2* Saw two stops.

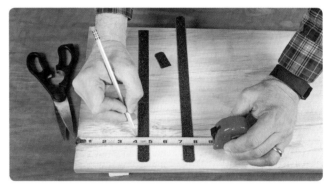

Fig. 4 Adhere anti-skid tape to the board.

Fig. 3 Glue and screw the stops to the board.

4. Optional: Paint your board.

5. Cut four strips of anti-skid tape a bit shorter than the width of the board. Adhere 2 strips at 4" (10 cm) and 7" (17.8 cm) from each end of the board *(Fig. 4)*.

6. Cut two pieces of vinyl traction tape long enough to wrap around the PVC pipe, so that the ends butt together and don't overlap.

7. Peel and carefully stick the tape 2" (5 cm) from each end of the roller *(Fig. 5)*. Done!

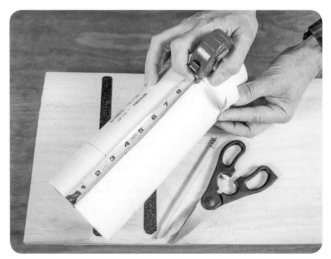

Fig. 5 Adhere vinyl traction tape to the roller.

ROLA BOLA

Rola bola involves balancing on top of a board on top of a roller. A big danger is when the board suddenly kicks out to the side *(Fig. 1)*. If the board kicks out, you could fall sideways and hurt your hip, wrist, or shoulder, and anyone next to you could get hit by the board. So make CERTAIN no one is next to you, *and ALWAYS use a spotter while learning.*

NOTE: Here's the link to our companion online tutorial on rola bola ABCs: www.DIYCircusLab.com/tutorials.

SAFETY FIRST!
- ROLA BOLA REQUIRES A SPOTTER. DO NOT ATTEMPT THIS ALONE.
- The spotter must be bigger than you, willing to use muscle to stop you from a sudden fall, and ready to catch your full body weight at any moment.
- Make sure the area is clear *all around you*.
- Practice on a carpet or mat to slow down the roller and soften a fall.
- Thank your spotter!
- Practice smart, practice safely!

Fig. 1 Board kick-out! Spotter, be alert!

The spotter should stand with feet apart and knees slightly bent. The spotter can be in front of you, holding your forearms with the circus grip *(Figs. 2 and 3)*, or behind you, holding onto your hip bones, or extending their arms under yours to guard you *(Fig. 4)*.

Fig. 2 Circus grip.

Fig. 3 Spotter's position from front. Fig. 4 Spotter's position from behind.

Circus posture is super important in all circus balance skills, with head over shoulders over hips. Imagine balancing a fishbowl on your head. Henry the goldfish lives in it. If you look down, Henry will crash to the floor! To save Henry from this misfortune, point your nose forward. Henry will thank you, and balancing will be easier (and safer).

STEP 1: MOUNT

Fig. 5 First foot on the board.

1. Put the board on the roller. Place one foot on the low side, near the end, with your toe pointing slightly outward *(Fig. 5)*.

2. Place your second foot on the high side, toe slightly outward.

3. *With your spotter's support*, bend your knees and skootch the board up on top of the roller. Center the board on the roller.

4. "Sit on the horse"—bent knees, bow legs, and torso long and tall. Don't lean on the spotter. Keep Henry the goldfish on your head by looking forward.

STEP 2: RIDE

1. With circus posture, work your legs by punching down with your feet. Keep your body centered over the roller. Hips and torso are still. All the action is in the legs. Check on Henry. This is a *moving* balance—you're never completely still.

STEP 3: DISMOUNT

1. Stop, pause, and roll to one side.

2. Step off. Remove Henry.

STEP 4: WEAN OFF THE SPOTTER

1. As you practice, pretend your spotter isn't there. Lighten your grip on your spotter, even lift off for a moment.

2. Then lift off a little longer—then for good. This takes time.

STEP 5: TAKE THE LEVEL 1 MASTERY TEST

The spotter stands behind, arms near your waist, not touching you unless needed.

1. Free-mount the board.

2. Balance for 20 seconds.

3. While *looking forward*, slowly squat down, touch the board, and slowly stand up again (*Fig. 6*).

4. While *looking forward*, slowly squat down, touch the floor, and slowly stand up again.

5. Dismount with *control* and *style*.

6. Thank your spotter!

When you can do these ABCs, you're ready for your Next Steps. See Resources on page 140.

Fig. 6 Touching the board for mastery.

TIE-ON STILTS

(!) Important! This design makes sturdy, lightweight stilts for beginner kids. At 12 inches (30.5 cm) high, the stilt bottom is reinforced by a foot support unit. Stilts that will be higher, or used with heavier kids, should be made of hardwood instead of pine. Note that board widths may vary (we ripped our boards to the actual dimensions shown here). Standard drywall screws, will split the wood, so use "self-drilling" screws, which require a special T-20 bit. Ask your local bike shop for a used bicycle tire for the treads.

TIME NEEDED
1–2 hours

MATERIALS

* speed square (optional)
* tape measure
* 10' (305 cm) length of 1"x3" clear pine (or about three 3' [1 m] pieces)
  (For taller stilts or heavier kids, use ash, hickory, or oak. No knots!)
* 2 sawhorses
* safety glasses
* crosscut (or power) saw (!)
* 4' (122 cm) length of 1" x 4" (2.5 x 10 cm) clear pine
* pencil
* scrap wood for drilling
* power drill with ⅛" (3 mm) drill bit and T-20 bit (!)
* wood glue
* 14 self-drilling screws, 2" (5 cm) long
* 4 self-drilling screws, 3" (7.5 cm) long
* tin snips (to cut bicycle tire)
* 20" (51 cm) old bicycle tire
* 4 washers
* 4 yards (4 m) slightly stretchy fabric
* kneepads (buy for later)

NOTE: Here's the link to our companion stilt-making tutorial: www.DIYCircusLab.com/tutorials.

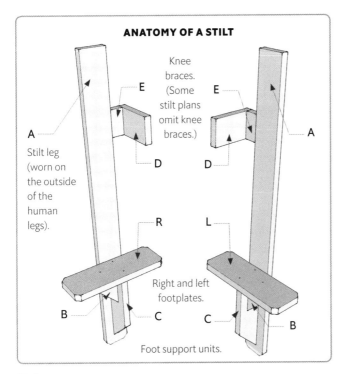

ANATOMY OF A STILT

Knee braces. (Some stilt plans omit knee braces.)

E

E

D

D

A

A

Stilt leg (worn on the outside of the human legs).

R

L

Right and left footplates.

B

C

C

B

Foot support units.

Fig.1

Fig. 4 Sub-assemble foot support units and footplates.

MAKE A PAIR OF STILTS

I. MEASURE, CUT & DRILL

1. From the 1" x 3" (2.5 x 7.5 cm) board, measure, cut, and drill holes as shown (*Figs. 1 & 2*) to create parts A–E.

2. From the 1" x 4" (2.5 x 10 cm) board, measure, cut, and drill holes as shown (*Fig. 3*) to create two footplates (R and L). Note that the holes mirror each other.

3. Cut corners off the footplates (R and L) and the bottoms of the legs (A).

II. ASSEMBLE

1. Sub-assemble foot support units B & C using glue and 2" (5 cm) screws. Add footplates R & L (*Fig. 4*). The units should mirror each other.

2. Draw lines for footplate placement:

   a. On each stilt leg A, draw a horizontal line 12" (30.5 cm) from floor.

   b. On each stilt leg, draw a vertical central line from floor to the 12" (30.5 cm) mark.

   c. Along the edges of the foot support units, mark centers to align with the central line on stilt leg A (*refer to Fig. 4*).

3. Using 2" (5 cm) screws, glue and screw foot units onto stilt legs under the 12" (30.5 cm) mark so they mirror each other (R and L). Note that Part B points to the front.

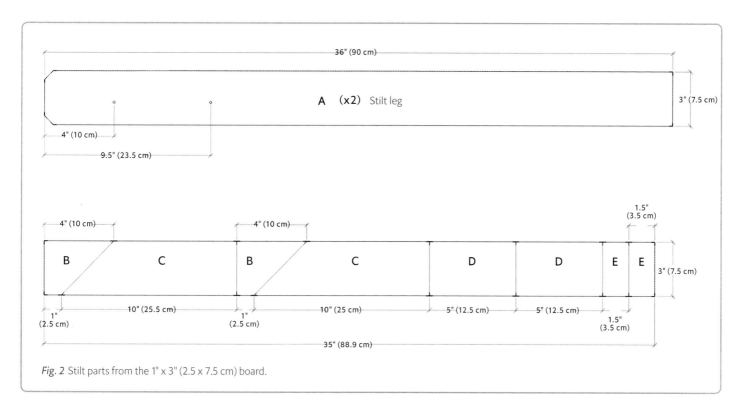

36" (90 cm)

A (x2) Stilt leg

3" (7.5 cm)

4" (10 cm)

9.5" (23.5 cm)

1.5" (3.5 cm)

4" (10 cm)

4" (10 cm)

B C B C D D E E

3" (7.5 cm)

1" (2.5 cm)

10" (25.5 cm)

1" (2.5 cm)

10" (25 cm)

5" (12.5 cm)

5" (12.5 cm)

1.5" (3.5 cm)

35" (88.9 cm)

Fig. 2 Stilt parts from the 1" x 3" (2.5 x 7.5 cm) board.

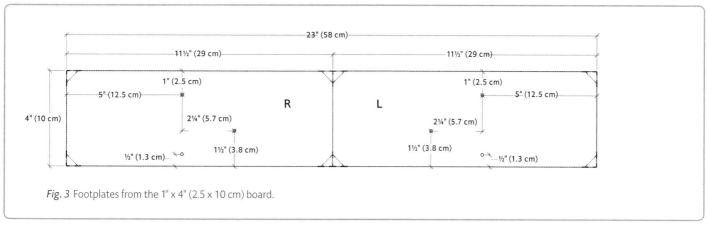

23" (58 cm)

11½" (29 cm)

11½" (29 cm)

1" (2.5 cm)

5" (12.5 cm)

R L

1" (2.5 cm)

5" (12.5 cm)

4" (10 cm)

2¼" (5.7 cm)

2¼" (5.7 cm)

½" (1.3 cm)

1½" (3.8 cm)

1½" (3.8 cm)

½" (1.3 cm)

Fig. 3 Footplates from the 1" x 4" (2.5 x 10 cm) board.

Fig. 5 Sub-assemble knee braces.

Fig. 6 Attach the knee braces.

Fig. 7 Secure the tire to the stilt.

4. Sub-assemble knee braces D & E with glue and 2" (5 cm) screws *(Fig. 5)*.

5. Using 3" (7.5 cm) screws, attach knee braces to the back edge of the stilt legs. Measure from child's own knee *(Fig. 6)*, placing braces low enough for the knee to bend past 90 degrees.

III. TREADS

1. Using tin snips, cut two pieces of bicycle tire, each 10" (25.4 cm) long.

2. Fold one piece into a U underneath one stilt leg. The edges can be folded over or cut off.

3. Use a washer and a 2" (5 cm) screw to fasten each end of the tire to the edge of the stilt leg *(Fig. 7)*.

4. Repeat on second stilt.

IV. TIES

1. Cut four fabric strips, 4 yards (4 m) x 3" (7.5 cm) wide *(Fig. 8)*.

Fig. 8 Cut the fabric straps.

STILT WALKING

SAFETY FIRST!
- The spotter must be bigger than you and able to stop or catch you from a sudden fall.
- You MUST wear knee pads. Check that ties are tight. Avoid slick or uneven surfaces. Check for hazards around you. And thank your spotter!
- Stilt walking takes time. Wean off the spotter gradually until you can pass the Level 1 test with confidence. Practice smart, practice safely!

NOTE: Here's the link to our companion online tutorial on the ABCs of stilt walking: www.DIYCircusLab.com/tutorials.

STEP 1: TIE IN

1. Put on sneakers and the kneepads. Find a high, stable spot to sit.

2. Tie in one foot, securing the toe, heel, and ankle with cross-over and cross-under tying *(Fig. 1)*. Hook the back of your sneaker to the footrest. Tie snugly without cutting off your circulation. End with a bow, avoiding your Achilles tendon.

3. Tie in under the knee *(Fig. 2)*. Make sure the knot is not under the kneecap.

4. Repeat on the other leg.

Fig. 1 Tie in the foot and ankle.

Fig. 2 Tie in the knee.

5. With your spotter, pull yourself to standing.

The spotter is in front of you. Hold each other's forearms with the circus grip *(Figs. 3 and 4)*. The spotter takes small steps backward as you walk forward. At first, your spotter might need to support you a LOT.

STEP 2: FORWARD, MARCH!

1. Sink your weight back into your heels. Check your circus posture!

2. Walk "on the spot"—shift your weight from one leg to the other, lifting your knees like you're marching.

3. Keep your knees apart, like a cowboy. Point your toes forward.

4. Start marching forward, *lifting your knees (Fig 5)*. (If you don't lift your knees you could trip yourself.) Walk around the room with your spotter.

STEP 3: EXPLORE WAYS OF WALKING (WITH SPOTTER!)

1. Step sideways: step, together, step. Both directions. Lift the knees.

2. Turn in a circle on the spot. Both directions. Lift the knees.

3. Walk backward with small steps. Lift the knees.

4. Step over a line on the floor, then low objects like a hoop or a stilt. Be sure to lift your BACK leg or you will trip. Spotter, be alert *(Fig. 6)*!

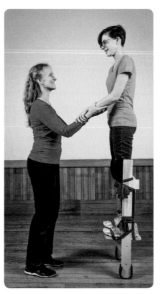

Fig. 4 Circus grip.

Fig. 3 Spotter's position.

Fig. 5 March with high knees.

Fig. 6 Step over the hoop.

STEP 4: PRACTICE FALLING

It's important to learn to fall to help prevent injuries should you actually fall while stilt walking.

1. Lay a mat or cushions on the floor.

2. Crouch low on the stilts, lean your chest back, gently drop to your knees (*Fig. 7*), and then bend forward, hands on the mat with your elbows bent and your fingers turned inward (*Fig. 8*). Do NOT drop straight down onto your knees.

3. Crawl on your hands and knees to a sturdy chair or table and (with your spotter) climb up to sitting. Check your ties, and retie them if they came loose.

STEP 5: TAKE THE LEVEL 1 MASTERY TEST

The spotter walks with you, arms up and ready, as you take your test, not touching you unless needed.

1. Tie in on your own. (Use help if necessary, but work toward doing it yourself.)

2. Ten steps forward.

3. Ten steps backward.

4. Five steps sideways, both directions.

5. Turn on the spot, both directions.

6. Step over the taped lines and low objects.

7. Fall, crawl, and pull yourself to sitting.

8. Remove your stilts and wrap them neatly.

9. Thank your spotter!

Fig. 7 Falling position #1.

Fig. 8 Falling position #2.

When you can do these ABCs on your own, you're ready for your Next Steps! See Resources on page 141.

TIGHTROPE

TIME NEEDED

45 minutes to make the X supports; 30 minutes to rig

MATERIALS

* two 6' (2 m) lengths of
  2" x 6" (5 x 15 cm)
  construction-grade pine
  (you can ask the lum-
  beryard to cut you four
  sections
  of 3' [1 m] each)
* 2 sawhorses
* tape measure
* pencil
* safety glasses (for power
  saw)
* handsaw or power saw (!)
* drill with ⅜" (9 mm) bit (!)
* 4 carriage bolts, 3½"–4"
  (9–10 cm) long, ⅜" (9 mm)
  diameter

* hammer
* 4 washers
* 4 hex nuts, ⅜" (9 mm)
  to match carriage bolts
* adjustable wrench
* 30'–40' (9–12 m) hemp rope,
  ¾" (2 cm).
  Important: The length of
  rope you need is based on
  the distance between, and
  the circumference of, the two
  trees. Allow enough extra
  rope to tie the knots.
* 2 sturdy trees, 10'–12'
  (3–4 m) apart

This rig requires two sturdy trees, so if you have an indoor circus you'll have to invite your audience outside for the tightrope act!

The hemp rope will stretch and loosen with use, so before each practice, make sure an adult checks your rigging to re-tension the rope.

NOTE: Here's the link to our companion online tutorial for making a tightrope: www.DIYCircusLab.com/tutorials.

MAKE THE X SUPPORTS

1. Place one of the 2" x 6" (5 x 15 cm) boards across two sawhorses. Measure and mark with pencil four 3' (1 m) lengths. Cut the pieces *(Fig. 1)*. (!)

2. To make the first X, take two of the 3' (91 cm) lengths and measure 26" (66 cm) from the end of each board. Mark it with a pencil.

3. Cross the boards at the 26" (66 cm) mark. This creates a wide span at the bottom of the X and a smaller span at the top. Adjust the boards to create a 12" (30.5 cm) distance across the smaller span *(Fig. 2)*.

Fig. 1 Saw the boards.

Fig. 2 Measure 12" (30.5 cm) across the top span.

4. Eyeball two bolt holes along the center line of the X. Drill the first hole through both boards, and tap a carriage bolt through with a hammer. Drill the second hole and tap another bolt through *(Fig. 3)*. (!)

5. Flip the X over. Add a washer and hex nut to each bolt, tightening firmly with the wrench.

6. Repeat to build a second X. Done!

Fig. 3 Tap the bolts through.

RIG THE TIGHTROPE ⓘ

Fig. 1 Tautline hitch around the anchor tree.

NOTE: You will need to learn to tie a tautline hitch, a trucker's hitch, and two half-hitches. We've provided some diagrams but also recommend www.netknots.com.

1. Wrap the rope around the first tree (your "anchor tree") as close to the ground as possible, just above the slant of the roots. Tie a tautline hitch, cinching the knot as close to the tree as possible *(Figs. 1 and 2)*.

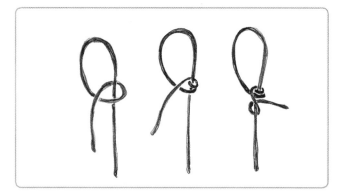

Fig. 2 Tautline hitch.

2. Lay down the Xs between the trees with the feet of each X about 3' (1 m) from each tree, and the tops of both Xs pointing toward the anchor tree. Extend the rope from the anchor tree over the Xs to the second tree (your "tension tree") *(Fig. 3)*.

Fig. 3 Set up the Xs and the rope between the trees.

3. Just above the feet of the X near the tension tree, tie the loop of the trucker's hitch *(Fig. 4)*. A second person holds this loop while you wrap the rope around the tree (low to the ground) and back through the loop. Pull tight *(Fig. 5)*!

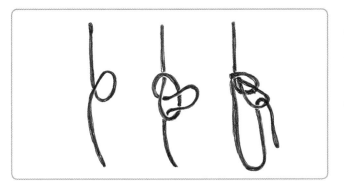

Fig. 4 Trucker's hitch.

> **NOTE:** To gain the most tension and reduce friction between the rope and the bark, you might need to put a plastic bag between the rope and the tree. This will allow it to slide as you tighten.

4. Finish off the trucker's hitch with two half-hitches *(Fig. 6)*.

5. With the rope as low and tight as possible, raise the two Xs and wedge them under the rope to maximize tension *(Fig. 7)*. Done!

6. With a spotter, carefully test the tension by stepping up on the rope. The rope should feel as tight as a cable.

> **NOTE:** (!) The rope will stretch as you use it. Before each practice session, you need to "re-tension" the rope:

1. Lay the Xs down.

2. Untie ONLY the two half-hitches.

> **NOTE:** Here's the link to our companion online tutorial: www.DIYCircusLab.com/tutorials.

Fig. 5 The trucker's hitch loop, pulling tight.

Fig. 6 Two half-hitch knots.

Fig. 7 Wedge the two Xs under the rope.

3. Pull the tail through the trucker's loop to tighten the rope.

4. Retie the two half-hitches and wedge the Xs back underneath. Good to go!

TIGHTROPE WALKING

SAFETY FIRST!

- **TIGHTROPE REQUIRES A SPOTTER. DO NOT ATTEMPT THIS ALONE.**
- The spotter can be any size if he or she is tall enough to reach your hand and strong enough to support you when you lose balance.
- Practice over grass or mats. Make sure the area is clear.
- Practice smart, practice safely!

NOTE: Here's the link to our companion online tutorial on tightrope walking ABCs: www.DIYCircusLab.com/tutorials.

Fig. 1 Spotter's position.

The spotter's position is at your side, slightly in front of you, an arm's distance away, with one hand raised in a fist. You hold the spotter's fist—the spotter doesn't hold you. The spotter *faces you*, walking backward as you walk forward *(Fig. 1)*.

Circus posture is super important in all circus balance skills. Imagine the fishbowl on your head containing Henry the goldfish, and don't let him slide off—keep your nose pointing forward, not down (even though you might want to look down very badly). Strive to keep your shoulders square—don't let them sway from side to side. Keep your torso centered over the rope.

STEP 1: WALKING ON THE GROUND

Before you get on the rope, practice walking on the ground in the special circus way:

1. Balancing on one foot, touch the big toe of your front foot to the big toe on the ground.

2. Slide your front foot along the imaginary rope and place it flat so your feet are in line.

3. Shift your weight to the front foot. Lift the back foot and move it in front, toe to toe.

4. Repeat the sequence: TOUCH, SLIDE, SHIFT.

Now try it on the rope.

STEP 2: WALKING ON THE ROPE

1. Hold the spotter's fist and carefully step up onto the rope.

2. *Lock your eyes* on the end of the rope. Use circus posture: Henry on your head, nose forward, arms up.

3. Holding the spotter's fist, slowly TOUCH, SLIDE, SHIFT (*Figs. 2, 3, and 4*).

4. Try a one-foot balance, extending one leg to the side. Balance on each leg.

Fig. 2 Toe-to-toe position on rope: TOUCH.

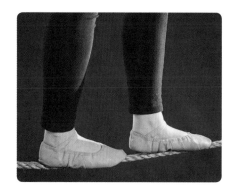

Fig. 3 SLIDE.

Fig. 4 SHIFT.

5. Walk to the end of the rope. Carefully step down. Style!

STEP 3: ARM POSITION

The arms are active in rope walking, not stuck out to the side like a scarecrow.

1. Lift your elbows near shoulder height, hands above your head.

2. Swipe your forearms side to side like windshield wipers *(Fig. 5)*.

3. Keep the shoulders square as much as possible—don't spill them sideways or they'll pull you off the rope.

Fig. 5 Wiper arms.

STEP 4: KNEELING

Once you have gained a little confidence, try kneeling—with your spotter.

1. From a one-foot balance, reach your free leg behind you and feel the rope with your toe. Slide your toe back along the rope to a lunge *(Fig. 6)*...

2. ...then lower your knee to the rope *(Fig. 7)*.

Fig. 6 Step back to a lunge...

Fig. 7 ...and then kneel.

STEP 5: WEAN OFF THE SPOTTER

As you're able, sense your balance as if the spotter weren't there. Lift off of your spotter's fist for a few seconds (spotter keeps the fist there, ready for you to grab it) *(Fig. 8)*. Gradually, lift off the spotter's fist for longer and longer periods, until you don't need it anymore. The spotter stays with you until you pass Level 1 Mastery—AND whenever you try something new on the rope.

STEP 6: TAKE THE LEVEL 1 MASTERY TEST

The spotter walks next to you, arm raised in a fist to grab onto, not touching you unless needed.

1. Step onto the rope.

2. Slide walk to the center. Arms are active, swiping side to side.

3. Balance for 5 seconds on each foot.

4. Kneel and stand.

5. Slide walk to the end.

6. Step off in full control. Style!

7. Thank your spotter!

When you can do these ABCs on your own, you're ready for your Next Steps! See Resources on page 140.

Fig. 8 One-foot balance, lifting off spotter.

A NOTE ABOUT FOOTWEAR

It's best to wear soft-soled shoes that allow you to feel the rope with your feet: ballet, martial arts, or water shoes—even bare feet. Thin-soled sneakers will also work, but we don't recommend thick-soled running shoes.

PARTNER ACROBATICS
and
HUMAN PYRAMIDS

Welcome to the art of climbing upon and holding up your fellow human beings!

Partner acrobatics are two-person forms, and pyramids use the same ideas but with three or more people. Different youth circuses have different names for these forms, so feel free to use what works for you.

Human pyramids look great when the humans wear hand-painted T-shirts. You might want T-shirts for your circus anyhow, so we're happy to show you how we made ours.

We love to end our circuses with a group pyramid act where each individual contributes to the unified whole!

Opposite: Circus Harmony: St. Louis Arches, St. Louis, MO. Credit: Greg Martin.

Introduction: ABOUT PYRAMIDS, CIRCADEMICS, AND CIRCUSSECRETS

Castellers in Barcelona.

Early evidence of human pyramid building dates back to a seventeenth-century Vietnamese wood carving and to an Italian print from 1652 of torch-bearing pyramid makers.

Human pyramids are performed today as a middle school sport in Japan, as entertainment by African troupes, and as a character-building activity of the Gymkana Troupe at the University of Maryland.

In Mumbai, India, pyramids are part of the Dahi Handi Festival to celebrate the birth of Lord Krishna. The goal is for team members (called *govindis*) to build a pyramid to reach a hanging pot (the *handi*) containing yogurt (*dahi*), dried fruit, and silver coins. Broken pieces of the pot itself are believed to ward off negative energy.

Perhaps the most famous human tower builders are the Castellers of Barcelona, who have competed since the eighteenth century to build the highest pyramids. The base (*pinya*) comprises a ring of the strongest men buttressed by a throng of people, upon whom lighter men create the middle layers (*manilles*). Next comes the tower (*tronc*) with children forming the tower dome (*pom de dalt*). The cherry on top (*enxaneta*) is a helmeted child who only stays long enough to raise one arm before the tower is carefully deconstructed. The human towers of Catalonia are safeguarded by the Convention of Intangible Cultural Heritage under the United Nations Educational, Scientific and Cultural Organization (UNESCO).

CIRCUSSECRETS:
Get Help, Give Help

The simple words "I need help" will summon a peer or an adult to support you when you're struggling with a new circus trick—but also when you're coping with a rough day at school or at home. Clear communication matters whether you're on the top or bottom of a ten-person pyramid *and* when you're feeling emotionally frazzled. The CircusSecret **get help** can make a big difference.

The flipside is when someone needs *your* help. Do you notice when someone is struggling? Have you ever asked, "Need help?" Someone might need a spotter or just a friendly ear to listen. Your teacher might need help cleaning up, or getting more co-operation and fewer putdowns from students. The CircusSecret **give help** can build trust, teamwork, and healthy relationships in your circus troupe and community.

CIRCADEMICS:
The Science
of Team Building

Pyramid making stands out as a top team-building activity where *everyone*, no matter how big or how small, makes a vital contribution to the overall goal. Pyramids involve taking risks, not just physically but also socially. Do you trust the person holding you up? Will the spotter keep you safe? Pyramids are built on trust, and trust starts with good communication.

Communication matters a lot in successful team building, and not just in circus. The *Harvard Business Review* says communication is the single most important thing to measure regarding group effectiveness, and the Human Dynamics Lab at MIT has created a scientific device to measure it. This device collects "sociometrics" on people's interactions, like tone of voice, face time, and how much they talk, listen, or interrupt. From this data they can look for patterns that make—or break—successful teamwork. It's so accurate they can predict which teams will win a business plan contest.

So maybe pyramid making could actually help prepare you for a successful career—even if it isn't in circus!

CIRCUS T-SHIRT

TIME NEEDED

1–2 hours, plus 24 hours dry time

MATERIALS

* copy of logo
* cardboard to protect table
* utility knife or scissors ⚠
* cardboard insert for shirt
* 1 prewashed T-shirt per trouper
* masking tape
* pencil or chalk
* fabric paints
* paintbrushes
* cup of water
* paper towels
* protective clothing

Having custom-made circus T-shirts will make your pyramids look infinitely more awesome. In fact, custom-made circus Ts will make your whole performance look more awesome. It's really about the T-shirts!

NOTE: Watch how our Circus Lab troupers painted their own T-shirts: www.DIYCircusLab.com/tutorials.

MAKE A CIRCUS T-SHIRT

1. Design a bold logo. Make copies *(Fig. 1)*.

2. Protecting the table with cardboard, use a utility knife or scissors to carefully cut a stencil *(Fig. 2)*. (!)

Fig. 2 Cut a stencil.

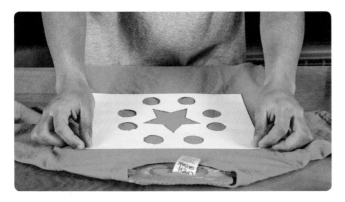

Fig. 3 Tape the stencil.

3. Slip the cardboard into the shirt, and tape the stencil in the upper center of the shirt *(Fig. 3)*.

4. Trace the logo lightly onto the shirt with pencil or chalk *(Fig. 4)*.

Fig. 1 Design a logo.

Fig. 4 Trace the logo.

Fig. 5 Paint the logo.

5. Remove the stencil and paint the logo *(Fig. 5)*.

6. Allow the paint to dry for at least 24 hours.

THE SECRET LANGUAGE OF PYRAMIDS

BASE, FLYER, SPOTTERS

In any group, people have different body sizes. YAY! Circus loves all sizes!

The **base** is the person who supports. The **flyer** is the person who climbs or is lifted. The **spotters** assist and safeguard the flyer (and sometimes the base).

Before you begin, be sure to warm up your wrists with easy circles, and gently stretch the backs of your legs.

KNEELING FORMS

- **Strong tabletop:** The base needs a long spine with a slight arch; straight, strong arms; shoulders aligned over wrists; and hips aligned over knees *(Fig. 1)*.
- **Weak tabletop:** The base should not have too much "cow" (belly sagging) or too much "cat" (back rounded) or be splayed too flat *(Fig. 2)*.

> **NOTE:** Here's the link to our companion online tutorial: www.DIYCircusLab.com/tutorials.

Fig. 1 DO make a strong tabletop.

Fig. 2 DON'T make a weak tabletop!

Fig. 3 DO stand on the "shelf." DON'T stand on the back!

Fig. 4 DO stack in alignment. DON'T be unsafe!

- **The shelf:** A proper tabletop creates a nice flat "shelf" for the flyer *(Fig. 3)*. *Flyers: Don't stand on the middle of the back or spine!*
- **Stacking alignment:** The flyer's hands should be on the base's shoulder blades, with a straight line of support from the flyer's shoulder down through the base's hands. Flyer places shins, not knees, on the shelf *(Fig. 4)*.

STANDING FORMS

- **"Sit on the horse":** The base stands with a tall spine, feet wide apart and angled slightly outward, knees bent deeply and angled over feet *(Fig. 5)*. Don't lean forward. Don't point your knees forward or inward.

Fig. 5 DO "sit on the horse." DON'T lean or turn knees inward!

- **The "pockets":** The flyer stands "on the pockets," high up where the leg and body join (*Fig. 6*). Don't ski down the thighs—ouch!

"HUP!"

"Hup!" is used by troupers everywhere to signal starting or stopping a trick, or changing position. You'll see how this works in the pyramid section. Decide who will call hups for each form.

THE "STYLE" (HEDGEHOGS AND GIRAFFES)

The only animals in our DIY circus are imaginary ones, like Norma the hedgehog and Bob the giraffe.

After you present a form, your "ta-da" moment is called a *style*. If you're kneeling, style with your arms down toward the little hedgehog on the floor (Norma); if you're standing, style with your arms up toward the big giraffe towering above you (Bob) (*Fig. 7*).

IMPORTANT POINTERS

- Plan the form ahead of time. Don't wait until someone is up to figure out how to get down.
- Pressure is not pain. Bases will feel pressure and sometimes discomfort, which is normal. Sharp pain or pressure beyond discomfort calls for an immediate *down*!
- "Down!" is the magic word. At the first sign of pain or imminent collapse, anyone can say *down*! Carefully dismantle the form, discuss what happened, then fix it and try again.
- Flyers: Never jump down—this pushes weight into the base (it hurts). Rather, *climb* down in reverse sequence, or drop off nice and easy using controlled movements.

Fig. 6 Flyers: DO stand high on thigh "on the pockets." DON'T ski down the thighs!

Fig. 7 "Style" up to Bob the giraffe, and down to Norma the hedgehog.

PARTNER ACROBATICS

Fig. 1 "Bench on a bench."

BENCH VARIATIONS FOR TWO PEOPLE

BENCH ON A BENCH (*Fig. 1*)
Spotter(s): Stand behind. Protect flyer from tipping backward or stepping on base.

1. Base assumes tabletop position.

2. Flyer places hands on base's shoulder blades, and gently places long surface of shins onto each side of the base's shelf. Do not dig knees into base's kidneys.

3. Look forward and smile!

4. Climb down and style.

CANDLE ON A BENCH (*Fig. 2*)
Spotter(s): Stand behind. Protect flyer from tipping backward or stepping on base.

SAFETY FIRST!

- PARTNER ACROBATICS REQUIRE AT LEAST ONE SPOTTER.
- The spotter must be bigger than you, willing to use muscle to stop you from falling, and ready to catch your full body weight at any moment.
- Practice on a mat or carpet.
- Review "The Secret Language of Pyramids" on pages 88–90. (Really!)
- Work together: listen, watch, get help, give help.
- Practice smart, practice safely!

NOTE: Here's the link to our companion online tutorial on partner acrobatic ABCs: www.DIYCircusLab.com/tutorials.

EQUIPMENT NEEDED: Gymnastic mats should be used.

1. Base assumes tabletop position.

2. Flyer puts hands on base's shoulder blades for support, then places a foot on base's shelf. Slowly add weight onto the shelf, then step up with second foot.

Fig. 2 Candle on bench.

Carefully stand. Spotter stands by to stabilize flyer.

3. Flyer styles to Bob.

4. Climb down in reverse sequence. Style!

SUPERHERO ON A BENCH *(Fig. 3)*
Spotter(s): Stand behind flyer to support in standing and protect from falling.

1. Base assumes tabletop position.

2. Flyer stands at the side of the base with one hand on a shoulder blade and one hand on base's shelf. Flyer places first foot on base's shelf, then gently steps up, placing second foot across both shoulder blades. Carefully stand and style.

3. Climb down in reverse sequence. Style!

"V" FOR VICTORY

In this form, partners counterbalance between a shared center of gravity. The flyer must FIRST step straight up, and THEN flyer and base extend arms and lean away from each other. Spotter(s): One spotter stands behind flyer. Hold hip bones to help into position. Second spotter stands behind base to protect from falling backward.

1. Base and flyer stand nose-to-nose, hands in circus grip, elbows bent. *(Fig. 4)*

2. With legs slightly apart and knees pointing forward, base squats slightly with straight back. Flyer places first foot

Fig. 3 Superhero on bench.

Fig. 4 Circus grip.

Fig. 5 V: Partners ready—circus grip, first foot up.

on base's thigh, just above the knee. Spotter is behind flyer *(Fig. 5)*.

3. On "Hup," flyer climbs *straight up* onto base as base supports flyer's arms upward. Both bodies are near vertical, close to an invisible center line with straight backs *(Fig. 6)*. If flyer bends and butt sticks out, flyer will pull base over. Push hips forward!

4. Base and flyer slowly extend their arms and lean back into a counterbalance *(Fig. 7)*. Do not collapse the chest—keep shoulders pulled down and back.

5. To come down, *first pull in* to center, *then* flyer drops down.

6. Style and smile!

There are a zillion ways to do partner acrobatics. The more you do them, the stronger and more flexible you'll get, which makes it possible to do more. Keep circusing!

Fig. 6 V: Flyer mounts straight up. Bodies close.

Fig. 7 V: Counterbalance, two hands.

HUMAN PYRAMIDS

SAFETY FIRST!
- **HUMAN PYRAMIDS REQUIRE SPOTTERS.**
- The spotter must be bigger than you, willing to use muscle to stop you from falling, and ready to catch your full body weight at any moment.
- Practice on a mat or carpet.
- Review "The Secret Language of Pyramids" on pages 88–90. (Really!)
- Work together: listen, watch, get help, give help.
- Practice smart, practice safely!

NOTE: Here's the link to our companion online tutorial on pyramid ABCs: www.DIYCircusLab.com/tutorials.

EQUIPMENT NEEDED: Gymnastic mats should be used.

THREE-PERSON CLASSIC STACK

Spotter: Stand behind flyer to protect from falling or stepping on bases' legs. Captain calls HUPs. Spotter stands behind flyer.

1. 1st HUP: Two bases drop to tabletop position, shoulders touching.

2. 2nd HUP: Flyer carefully kneels atop the two bases—right shin across right base's shelf, right hand on right base's shoulder blade. Mirror on left base.

Fig. 1 Three-person classic stack, flyer kneeling.

3. Look forward and smile *(Fig. 1)*!

4. 3rd HUP: Come down. Flyer *carefully* steps down to the back. DO NOT STEP on the bases!

5. Bases kneel and style to Norma, flyer stands and styles to Bob.

VARIATION 1: STANDING CLASSIC STACK
Spotter: Stand behind flyer to protect from falling or stepping on bases' legs. Lend stability.
- Same as above, except flyer shifts from shins to feet and slowly stands on bases' shelves. Style and smile *(Fig. 2)*.
- Spotter lends stability and guards against falling backward.
- To come down, flyer carefully returns to shins and then dismounts.
- Style to Bob and Norma.

Fig. 2 Three-person classic stack, flyer standing.

Fig. 3 Infinite classic stack!

VARIATION 2: INFINITE CLASSIC STACK *(Fig. 3)*

More spotters are needed as the pyramid grows. Stand behind flyers who most need help or bases who need coaching.

- Same as above, except with multiple bases and flyers. Practice in sections first, and then put the whole pyramid together. This works with any number of people.
- Bases now support two flyers, one on each side.
- Everyone moves at the same time, according to Hups.
- Anyone can call "down" if something needs fixing.

THREE-PERSON THIGH FLY

Spotter: Stand behind flyer. Support in stepping up, and help stabilize. Captain calls Hups.

1. Two bases stand next to each other, feet wide apart and turned slightly outward, pinky toes touching. Flyer stands behind with a hand on each shoulder.

2. Captain calls "Ready!" Bases bend their knees ("sit on the horse"), with straight backs. Flyer places right foot onto base's "pocket." Base holds foot in place. *(Fig. 4)* Flyer's foot needs to be right next to the base's body. If the foot slides down the base's leg, it will hurt the base.

3. 1st HUP: Flyer steps up onto right base's pocket by *pushing down* on both bases' shoulders. Bases resist. Flyer *must not pull back* on shoulders. Flyer puts left foot onto left base's pocket and stands tall. Bases hook their arms through the flyer's legs and hold snugly just above the knee.

4. Style and smile for 5 seconds *(Fig. 5)*.

5. 2nd HUP: Come down. Bases must *release flyer's legs*. Then flyer drops forward to ground and kneels. Flyers: Drop down easy; do NOT jump off the bases.

6. Flyer styles Norma, and bases style Bob.

VARIATION: INFINITE THIGH FLY

Same as above, except with multiple bases and flyers. Practice in sections first and then put the whole pyramid together. This works with an unlimited number of people. More spotters are needed as the pyramid grows. Place spotters where most needed.

- This pyramid is more stable on a curved line. Anyone can call "down" if something needs fixing.

Fig. 4 Three-person thigh fly: Ready.

Fig. 5 Three-person thigh fly.

Fig. 6 Infinite thigh fly: Ready.

Fig. 7 Infinite thigh fly!

- Bases are now supporting two flyers, one on each side. Therefore, all flyers must start with the same foot *(Fig. 6)*.
- All flyers must push down on bases' shoulders and *must not pull back*.
- Everyone moves at the same time, according to hups *(Fig. 7)*.
- Bases must *release flyers' legs* before flyers dismount.
- Style to Bob and Norma!

FOUR-PERSON GERMAN STACK

I call this the German stack because I first saw it performed by the Circus Calibastra in Stuttgart, Germany. Circus Smirkus calls it the Zipper.

No HUPs are needed; simply take turns getting into position. This pyramid adds a "middle" and a "top flyer" (your smallest trouper). Spotter moves between flyer and top flyer.

Spotters stand behind flyer and top flyer, protecting them from falling.

1. Base takes tabletop position.

2. Middle faces base and leans forward, hands on base's shoulder blades.

3. Flyer carefully steps up onto base's shelf and leans on middle's shoulders *(Fig. 8)*.

4. Top flyer climbs onto the middle's shelf with spotter's help:
   • Middle extends one leg back to create a step for the top flyer.
   • Top flyer holds middle's torso and places a foot on the middle's calf, close to the knee bend *(Fig. 9)*. On "hup" the middle gently pops the knee to boost the top flyer up, while top flyer pushes up at the same time onto middle's shelf. Spotter holds top flyer's waist and helps lift.
   • Top flyer leans with hands on flyer's shoulders.

5. Look out and smile for 5 seconds *(Fig. 10)*.

6. With spotter's help, climb down in reverse order. Do NOT jump. Style to Bob and Norma.

> **NOTE:** For an awesome eight-person German stack, go to our online videos! www.DIYCircusLab.com/tutorials.

Fig. 8 Three-person German stack.

Fig. 9 Top flyer prepares to step onto middle's calf.

Fig. 10 Four-person German stack.

COW PYRAMID (WITH 10 COWS)

The Flying Gravity Circus invented the crazy cow names for this pyramid. See their awesome 21-Cow pyramid on page 12!

- Anyone can call "down" if something needs fixing.
- Everyone moves in layers, according to hups:

1. 1st HUP: "Ground Beef"—four bases in tabletop with space between them.

2. 2nd HUP: "Lean Beef"—three standers stand between bases, hands on bases' shoulder blades, backs arched to create a flat shelf.

3. 3rd HUP: "Flying Cows"—two Flying Cows step up onto bases' shelves, hands on their shoulder blades.

4. 4th HUP: "Cherry Cow on Top" is lifted by a spotter onto the shelf of the central stander. Stander arches back to create a flat shelf.

5. Look forward and smile for 5 seconds (Fig. 11).

6. Spotter lifts Cherry Cow off. Descend in reverse order. Careful of Ground Beef's legs. Style!

There are a million ways to make pyramids. The stronger and more flexible you become, the more options you'll have for climbing on and supporting your friends in fun and safe ways! See Resources on page 140.

Fig. 11 Ten-person cow pyramid.

UNIT 5

CLOWNING

Welcome to clowning!

While the circus performer makes a hard trick seem easy, an easy trick for the clown is so hard! Just walking across the floor, the clown trips . . . or putting on a hat, it pops off. Props don't behave for a clown the way they do for ordinary people!

"The little red nose is the smallest mask in the world," said master clown Jacques LeCoq. You can make your own—and a hat that does tricks, too—to start discovering your inner clown.

Opposite: Clowns from Circus Smirkus, Greensboro, VT.

There are many books about clowning (I've listed some good ones for you in the Resources section). Visit a library and ask for them. Or look up any of these words: *Fool*, *Jester*, *Trickster*, *Hayoka*, *Zany*, *Commedia dell'Arte*, *Harlequin*, or *Auguste Clown*.

But here's what I'd like to tell you now: Clowns were not invented to sell hamburgers, or to creep people out. Clowns exist because human beings need them. We know this is true because they've existed throughout time, everywhere on earth. Why is this so?

Historically, clowns confuse things, get things backward, and do things that are contrary to what normal people do. We stress out about dressing cool—meanwhile, the clown's pants fall down. If that happened to you, it would be bad, right? But we laugh at the clown.

Floyd Shaffer, author of *Clown Ministry*, says, "When you take something that is painful or 'bad' and expand it dispro-portionately, it becomes funny. Laughing at painful things makes them a bit more bearable."

Remember your last really big belly laugh? And how good you felt afterward? Science shows that laughing reduces stress, decreases pain, lowers blood pressure, and boosts the immune system (these effects are facts, researchers measured this). Somehow, we've always known that laughter is good for us, but we need to do it more—not easy in this super-serious world. Clowns make us laugh, and so they make us well. We need clowns now more than ever!

CIRCUSSECRETS: Watch, Listen

To learn circus, you need the CircusSecrets **watch** and **listen**. If you *really watch* how the sticks are held or the exact motion of the arms, and you *really listen* to the teacher's spoken (or the book's written) words, you will learn better.

When you're with other people, are you aware how they're feeling? When you *really notice* your fellow troupers, you can spot clues that something's up—like when your friend stands apart from the group with crossed arms, scowling. If you *really listen*, you can tell how someone's really feeling—like when they say they're okay, but they're not. Under-standing other people's feelings is called *empathy*, and it's good to practice it—in circus and in life.

CIRCADEMICS:
Clowning as Medicine

The Laughter League at Children's Health, Dallas, TX. Credit: Hannah Henderson.

When kids are about to have surgery, they feel really anxious. Research shows that anxiety before surgery can lead to problems recovering even six months later, so it's important to help kids calm down before their operations. Doctors can give children medication to relax them, but sometimes those drugs have side effects. So hospitals need ways to reduce children's anxiety without drugs. Enter the clowns.

Certain hospitals have Clown Care teams that use humor and play to help kids get well. It's serious business. Medical clowns are specially trained in therapeutic techniques, working alongside doctors and nurses to support young patients who don't have much to laugh about. They visit children in their hospital rooms to cheer and empower them. And they help kids calm down before surgery—really.

Researchers in four countries have found that kids who were "clowned" before surgery had less anxiety than kids who were given drugs. Just think about that—being with clowns worked better than medication! It's true—you can look this up in medical journals. And it worked on the parents, too. Now that's something to smile about.

"Creepy" Clowns

REAL clowns are respected professional artists. REAL clowns study clowning, work from the heart, love their job, and want to brighten people's lives. Creepy "clowns" are not clowns. They're phony, attention-seeking imposters or actors in horror films. It's easy to tell the difference—please don't judge real clowns by the fakes. Support REAL clowns!

CLOWN NOSE

TIME NEEDED

1 hour, plus overnight drying time, plus a little more...

MATERIALS

* 2 kinds of absorbent paper (like paper towels, brown and white)
* 1 Styrofoam ball 1½"–2" (4–5 cm)
* plastic wrap
* small bottle of Elmer's glue
* small bowl or cup
* inexpensive paintbrush
* clothespin or paper clip
* butter knife
* scissors (with sharp point)
* red acrylic paint or red magic marker
* thin elastic cord, 18" (46 cm) long
* liquid cosmetic foundation in your skin tone (optional)

This top-secret recipe makes an *awesome* clown nose! A good shnozz should be full and round, not a half-ball. (Our Nose Technicians discovered the secret: a Styrofoam ball. Shh!)

NOTE: Here's the link to our companion online tutorial for making a clown nose: www.DIYCircusLab.com/tutorials.

MAKE A CLOWN NOSE

PREPARATION

1. Make two piles of differently colored paper towels. Tear (don't cut) the paper into small pieces.

2. Cover the Styrofoam ball with plastic wrap. Twist the wrap closed so you have something to hold onto.

3. Pour 2–3 tablespoons (30–45 ml) of glue into a bowl. Add a little water and stir it into the glue.

Fig. 1 Layers in process.

Fig. 2 Pull out plastic wrap.

LAYER AND DRY

1. Paint a small area of the ball with glue. Lay a piece of paper towel on top and paint over it with more glue *(Fig. 1)*.

2. Cover most of the ball with one color paper, overlapping the edges. (Tip: You can use the paintbrush to pick up the paper, rather than your fingers.) Don't cover the area around the twisted plastic wrap—leave that area open.

3. Repeat the process with the second color (so you can see what you've covered).

4. Continue to alternate paper until you've glued on six to eight layers.

5. Hang the ball with clothespins or paper clips to dry overnight.

HOLLOW OUT AND REINFORCE

1. The next day (or when the ball is completely dry), untwist the plastic wrap to expose the Styrofoam.

2. Using a butter knife, carefully carve out the Styrofoam. Remove the plastic wrap *(Fig. 2)*.

3. With sharp scissors, trim the edge of the nose so the opening is oval *(Fig. 3)*.

4. Use the scissors to *carefully* carve out two holes for nostrils. (!)

Fig. 3 Trim the edge.

5. With glue and brush, reinforce the edge of the nose with two extra layers, bending paper over the edge and gluing it inside and outside. Allow it to dry for at least 2 hours.

PAINT AND TIE

1. When the nose is dry, paint or color it red. Allow to dry.

2. Use scissors to *carefully* bore two pinholes on either side of the nose for the elastic *(Fig. 4)*. ⓘ

3. Measure a length of elastic around your head, allowing extra for knots.

4. Tie one end through one pinhole. Measure around your head and tie the elastic to the second hole. Snip off the extra.

5. Dab red paint to hide the elastic on the nose. Optional: Rub skin-colored liquid makeup into the elastic to help camouflage it on your face.

6. Try it on *(Fig. 5)*!

Fig. 4 Carefully bore holes for the elastic.

Fig. 5 Clown noses ready for action!

CLOWN HAT

TIME NEEDED

1 hour or so

MATERIALS

* 2 lengths of foam pipe insulation, 6' (2 m) long, with one hole diameter of ½" (1.3 cm)
* scissors
* 2 yards (2 m) of light-duty chain (to give the hat weight)
* needle-nose pliers (optional)
* 1 roll of duct tape (black is traditional)
* colored tape, for hatband (optional)

The Hat Technicians in our Circus Lab designed this funky hat that flips nicely. (The secret is the chain in the brim for extra weight. Shh!) Make it just a little big for your head so the tricks work better.

NOTE: Here's the link to our companion online tutorial for making a hat: www.DIYCircusLab.com/tutorials.

MAKE A CLOWN HAT

THE BRIM

1. Wrap a length of pipe insulation around your head, adding an extra 1" (2.5 cm) so the hat is a bit big for you. Cut the pipe insulation, but don't tape it yet.

2. Measure and cut two or three strands of chain as long as the pipe insulation. (To "cut" the chain, pry the links apart with scissors or pliers.) Tape the ends of the chains together (Fig. 1).

Fig. 1 Pipe and chains measured.

3. Slip the chains into the pipe insulation (Fig. 2). Tape the two ends of the chain together in a ring, then close the pipe insulation into a ring by taping the ends together.

Fig. 2 Slip the chains into the pipe.

4. Slice a length of pipe insulation in half the long way. Cut a length that fits around the brim.

Fig. 3 Add a circle of half pipe and tape the brim.

5. Tape it around the outside of the brim (to make it a little wider). Cover the entire brim with tape (Fig. 3).

THE CROWN

1. Slice two more lengths of pipe insulation the long way.

2. Form a ring that is just a bit smaller than the brim. Tape the ends together.

3. Repeat to form two or three more rings. (The more rings, the taller the crown.)

4. Stack them and tape them to each other, but not to the brim yet (Fig. 4).

Fig. 4 The crown in the making.

Fig. 5 Form the top of the crown.

Fig. 7 Tape the crown to the brim.

THE TOP

1. Cut a piece of sliced-open pipe to fit across the top, and two shorter pieces to make a cross (*Fig. 5*).

2. Cut four more short pieces of pipe to fill in the gaps, like "pieces of pie."

3. Tape the pie pieces to the top ring and to each other (*Fig. 6*).

4. Cover the top with tape, closing the holes.

Fig. 6 "Pieces of pie" filling in the top.

ATTACH THE BRIM TO THE CROWN

1. Tape the brim to the crown. Tip: Cut tape as shown for the tricky joint where the crown meets the brim (*Fig. 7*).

2. Cover any exposed pipe insulation with tape.

3. Try it on!

4. Optional: Add a stripe of colored tape for a hatband.

CLOWNING

NOTE: Here's the link to our companion online tutorial on clowning: www.DIYCircusLab.com/tutorials.

FACIAL AEROBICS

Showing expressions with your face is one way to wake up the clown inside you.

1. Find a mirror and put on your nose.

2. Admire yourself for 30 seconds. You're the world's best-looking clown!

3. Squinch your face as small as possible. Open your face as big as possible.

Fig. 1 Aerobics #1: mouth up, eyebrows up.

Fig. 2 Aerobics #2: mouth up, eyebrows down.

Fig. 3 Aerobics #3: mouth down, eyebrows down.

Fig. 4 Aerobics #4: mouth down, eyebrows up.

4. Practice *facial aerobics*. It goes like this:

   a. Put your mouth up and eyebrows up *(Fig. 1)*.
   b. Keep your mouth up, put your eyebrows down *(Fig. 2)*.
   c. Keep your eyebrows down, put your mouth down *(Fig. 3)*.
   d. Keep your mouth down, put your eyebrows up *(Fig. 4)*.
   e. Repeat!

5. Add your whole body to lots of expressions: happy, sad, mad, surprised, disgusted, afraid.

GAME: WHAT IS THIS THING?

Put some random props around the room (hoop, umbrella, plunger, feather duster, etc.).

1. Pretend that you've just arrived from another planet. You've never seen any earthly objects before and have no idea what they're for.

2. With childlike curiosity, *explore this thing*. Drop it, throw it, balance it, put it on your head. Play! After a minute or two, find another object to explore *(Fig.5)*.

Fig. 5 Clowns exploring different props simultaneously.

GAME: WHAT IT ISN'T
(OR: USES IN A MINUTE)

This game is more fun with more people. Players take turns using a prop in different ways *except* what it's actually for. (An umbrella is a sword, guitar, or pony—but not something to keep off the rain.) Note: Keep gestures and language appropriate!

1. Players stand in a circle around one prop.

2. Player runs to the center, does something with the prop for 5 seconds, drops it, and runs back to the circle.

3. Take turns in rapid fire. Do as many ideas as you can in a minute.

4. After a minute, switch props.

TRIPPING OVER YOUR OWN FEET

Knowing how to trip (accidentally on purpose) is a classic clown skill. So are the double-take and the report.

1. Walk along, minding your own business.

2. Catch one foot behind the heel of the other, fall forward, and then catch yourself *(Fig 6)*. Hide the tricky part from the audience *(Fig. 7)*.

3. STOP, point your toes toward, the audience, and . . .

4. Do a double-take (see below) and . . .

5. Report to the audience (see below).

Fig. 6 Act of tripping—clown falling forward.

Fig. 7 Foot hooked behind heel.

Fig. 8 Casually look back.

Fig. 9 Casually look at camera.

Fig. 10 Look quickly back.

Fig. 11 Report surprise!

THE "DOUBLE-TAKE"

In physical comedy, a "take" is a reaction to something. A "double-take" is when you look, then look again, and react to what you see. With good timing it'll get a laugh every time.

In this case, after you trip:

1. *Casually* notice what you tripped over *(Fig. 8)* . . .

2. *Casually* look at the audience *(Fig. 9)*, then suddenly . . .

3. *Look quickly* back where you tripped *(Fig. 10)*, and finally . . .

4. *REPORT (Fig. 11)*!

THE "REPORT"

To report means to look smack at the audience and show your reaction: facial expression, body language, everything.

In this case, after your double-take:

1. Report SURPRISE that you just tripped. OR:

2. Report JOY that you tripped over a $100 bill! OR:

3. Report FEAR that you tripped over a rattlesnake! OR:

4. Report DISGUST that you tripped over stinky garbage! OR:

5. You get the idea!

FUN WITH YOUR HAT

NOTE: Here's the link to our companion online tutorial on hat tricks: www.DIYCircusLab.com/tutorials.

Making your hat pop up, skid across the floor, and flip up to your hand are classic hat tricks that should be in every clown's back pocket.

THE POP UP

In this trick, just as you put the hat on, it "magically" pops off your head!

1. The motion—without the tricky part—is to simply put the hat on your head. Hold the hat with both hands, raise it high over your head with straight arms, and pull it down onto your head.

2. Now for the tricky part. Put the hat aside for a moment. With each hand, make a circle with your middle fingers and thumb (*Fig. 1*). Flick your middle fingers off your thumb with a quick, sharp movement (*Fig. 2*).

3. Pick up the hat and hold the brim as shown (*Fig. 3*). Flick the hat with your middle fingers.

4. Put it all together:
   - Hold the hat with both hands, secretly preparing your tricky fingers on the brim.
   - Raise the hat with straight arms high above your head (*Fig. 4*).

Fig. 1 Make circles with your thumb and middle fingers.

Fig. 2 Flick your fingers open.

Fig. 3 Hold the hat with finger circles.

Fig. 4 Hat raised, tricky fingers ready.

- Bend your elbows, and *the moment* the hat touches your head, pop your fingers. The hat flies off *(Fig. 5)*!

Fig. 5 The pop!

TIPS

- When you pop the hat, *keep your hands next to your head as you flick your fingers*. Don't move your hands up or the audience will know it was you.
- WAIT until the hat hits the ground—THEN report your surprise!

THE RUNAWAY HAT

In this trick, the hat has fallen on the floor. Just as you bend down to pick it up, it scoots away!

1. Start with the hat on the floor. Step up so your toe is just touching the brim *(Fig. 6)*.

Fig. 6 Hat on floor, first foot touching brim.

2. Start to reach down *just as* you slide your second foot next to the first. Secretly bump the hat with your toe so it skids forward *(Fig. 7)*. This secret bump is the tricky part.

Fig. 7 The secret bump (the tricky part).

3. When the hat skids away, keep your hand reaching down to where the hat *was*. But follow the hat with your *nose* *(Fig. 8)*. Then report to the audience ("Huh?") *(Fig. 9)*.

TIPS

- Hide the tricky part from the audience. Turn sideways so you hide the foot that bumps the hat.
- Don't KICK the hat—the audience should not see any extra foot motion that shows you did it. Simply bring your second foot up to the first and bump the hat.
- Bump the hat at the *same moment* you bend over and reach down.

Fig. 8 Follow the hat with your nose, not your hand.

Fig. 9 Report: "Huh?"

THE FLIP UP

In this trick, you toss your hat—which flips gently once in the air—into your upraised hand.

1. Bend your favorite arm to a 90-degree angle, holding the elbow next to your body. Your hand is flat, palm up. Hang the hat on the fingers only. Don't hold the brim with your thumb.

2. Raise your other arm straight up over your head. Hold the raised hand like a wide-open duck's beak, with your thumb sticking forward *(Fig. 10)*.

3. Keeping your elbow next to your body, make a gentle down-up motion by lowering your forearm and swiftly lifting it—then STOP. The hat should fly off your hand with a nice easy spin (one revolution) *(Fig. 11)*.

4. Looking *straight ahead*, gently flip the hat up to the duck hand and grab it. Ta-da *(Fig. 12)*.

TIPS
- Don't use your thumb—keep it next to your palm.
- Don't flick your wrist; your hand and forearm are a unit.
- Look straight ahead, not at the hat.

These hat tricks are just the tip of the iceberg in a clown's tool chest. Keep learning! See the Resources on page 140.

Fig. 10 Ready position: hat on flat hand, duck arm ready.

Fig. 11 The hat flies off your hand.

Fig. 12 Duck catches the hat—but don't look!

RUNNING GAG

Fig. 1 Alpha produces small hanky from small hat.

Fig. 2 Beta wants to try! "Pleeeeeeease?"

A *running gag* is a clown act that reappears throughout the circus, building to a final surprise punchline (the "blow-off") near the end of the show. The reappearance of the clowns in the same situation increases the comic effect. The audience welcomes the clowns like old friends, anticipating what will happen next.

We usually stick to the magic number three—three appearances—because, for reasons that remain a timeless mystery, comedy works in threes.

THE THREE MAGIC HATS (FOR 2 CLOWNS)

Two clowns: Alpha and Beta

Props: 1 small hat, 1 medium hat, 1 tall hat (make your own or find), 2 small handkerchiefs, 2 medium handkerchiefs, 1 large handkerchief, 2 identical pairs of socks, 1 pair of boxers, and 2 clown noses, of course!

> **NOTE:** This gag can be performed with or without words. If you are doing it without words, act out the written lines with gestures and mime them instead of speaking them.

NOTE: Here's the link to our companion online tutorial showing the running gag: www.DIYCircusLab.com/tutorials.

GAG #1: SMALL HAT

ENTER Alpha wearing the small hat, with Beta (no hat) following like a puppy.

Alpha prepares to do a magic trick: Removes small hat, makes magical gestures/says magical words, and—*voilà*! Pulls out a small handkerchief *(Fig. 1)*. Bows proudly.

Beta reports amazement. Then (spoken or mimed):

Beta: Hey, can I try?

Alpha: No.

Beta: Can I try, please?

Alpha: NO!

Beta: Pretty pleeeeeeeeeease? *(Fig. 2)*

Alpha: Oooohhh . . . all right.

Beta takes small hat, imitates Alpha's preparation for the magic trick. Makes same magical gestures/words, and—*voilà*! Pulls out a small handkerchief . . . is tied to a sock *(Fig. 3)*.

Beta reports surprise. Hands hat to Alpha. Looks down, pulls up right trouser leg, revealing a similar sock. Pulls up left trouser leg, which is bare. Reports alarm—how'd that happen? *(Fig. 4)*

Alpha laughs and exits. Beta scratches head and follows Alpha.

Fig. 3 Beta produces . . . a sock.

Fig. 4 "Hey!"

GAG #2: MEDIUM HAT

ENTER Alpha wearing the medium hat, with Beta (no hat) following like a puppy.

Alpha prepares to do a magic trick: Removes medium hat, makes magical gestures/says magical words, and—*voilà*! Pulls out a medium handkerchief *(Fig. 5)*. Bows proudly.

Beta reports amazement. Then (spoken or mimed):

Beta: Hey, can I try?

Alpha: No.

Beta: Can I try, please?

Alpha: NO!

Beta: Pretty pleeeeeeeeease? *(Fig. 6)*

Alpha: Oooohhh... all right.

Beta takes medium hat, imitates Alpha's preparation for the magic trick. Makes same magical gestures/words, and—*voilà*! Pulls out a medium handkerchief... which is tied to another sock *(Fig. 7)*.

Beta reports surprise. Hands hat to Alpha. Looks down, pulls up trouser legs—both legs are bare. Reports alarm—what, again? *(Fig. 8)*

Alpha laughs and exits. Beta reports frustration, follows Alpha in a huff.

Fig. 5 Alpha produces medium hanky from medium hat.

Fig. 6 Beta REALLY wants to try!

Fig. 7 Beta produces... another sock.

Fig. 8 "What, AGAIN?"

Fig. 9 "Look what I found!"

Fig. 10 Alpha accuses Beta.

Fig. 11 Alpha REALLY wants to do the magic trick.

GAG #3: TALL HAT

ENTER Beta, alone, wearing tall hat: "Lookkit what I have!" *(Fig. 9)*. Looks carefully around but doesn't see Alpha.

Beta prepares to do a magic trick: Removes tall hat, makes magical gestures—

ENTER Alpha, searching for the tall hat. Sees Beta—"HEY!" *(Fig. 10)*

Beta stops. Then (spoken or mimed):

Alpha: Gimme my hat!

Beta: No.

Alpha: Gimme my hat!!

Beta: NO!

Alpha: Pretty pleeeeeeeeeease? *(Fig. 11)*

Beta: Oooohhh . . . all right.

Beta holds the tall hat toward Alpha, who prepares for the magic trick as before. Makes same magical gestures/ words, and—*voilà!* Pulls out a large handkerchief . . . which is tied to a pair of boxers *(Fig. 12)*.

Alpha reports surprise. Holds boxers in front of waist. Reports alarm—Oh no!

Beta laughs, takes hat—and runs off with Alpha chasing.

Fig. 12 Surprise ending!

MAKING

a

SHOW

Welcome to show making!

This is where you pull it all together. You've already worked hard making the props and learning the skills. Now, take what you know and link it together . . .

. . . with your friends! You all get to decide how you want your circus to be, the theme and the music, where to perform, whom to perform for, and everything. Can your circus help a cause? You da boss. You can do it.

So here we go—Hup*Hey!

Opposite: The Circus Lab Troupers.

Introduction: ABOUT THE TOOLBOX FOR WORKING TOGETHER AND CIRCUSSECRETS

Fig. 1 The council club.

There's an important circus skill we haven't discussed yet: how to work together. It really is a skill that takes practice.

When people collaborate, competing ideas, leadership struggles, and arguments often upset the process. Use these tools to smooth the way. And if you want to have a theme for your circus, use the same brainstorming and dot-voting process shown here.

FORM A CIRCLE

The circle is a time-honored meeting space, and the "ring" has always been a special space among circus people. For group conversations and reflections, we recommend making a circle so every voice can be heard.

To help the group stay focused, place something in the middle that relates to the conversation.

Use a talking stick as a reminder not to interrupt the speaker *(Fig. 1)*. (In the old Circus Smirkus council meetings, Smirkos used a juggling club for their "Council Club.")

SET YOUR AGREEMENTS

Before you build your circus, make time to set your agreements: a code of conduct for working together that everyone creates and agrees on. This is an important tool for uniting the group, reducing problems later, or stopping problems before they begin.

NOTE: Here's the link to our online Toolbox tutorial: www.DIYCircusLab.com/tutorials.

CIRCUSSECRETS:
Stop, Think, and Choose, and Reflect

Use the CircusSecret **stop, think, and choose** when something wrong or unsafe happens. First, STOP whatever's happening and think about how or why it happened. Ask what the options could have been and what the better choice is going forward.

Practice the CircusSecret **reflect** at the end of every class or session. Allow time to honestly consider these two thoughts: 1.) What went well? 2.) It would be even better if . . .

MATERIALS

* 3" x 5" (7.5 x 12.7 cm) index cards
* pens
* sticker dots
* paper
* laminator

1. Ask yourselves: What things are important to do or say (or not do, not say) when working in a group?

2. Break into smaller groups for about 10 minutes (time-keeper needed). Each group brainstorms five to eight suggestions, writing one suggestion per index card. (Examples: No put-downs. Use equipment properly.)

3. Return to the circle and share the suggestions. Merge similar ideas. Reflect and discuss.

4. Post the index cards in categories on a wall. Hand out up to eight sticker dots to each person. Each person votes one dot for their top choices ("dot voting") *(Fig. 2)*. Select agreements with the most votes.

5. Write out the agreements, laminate them, and post them. Review them before each session.

SAY "OUCH"

People can say mean things—sometimes accidentally, sometimes on purpose. If no one speaks up, it usually happens again.

If you witness someone getting "dissed," simply say, "Ouch!" *(Fig. 3)*. This statement tells the person who spoke meanly that you heard it—and it hurt. It also tells the person who was dissed that you support them. Of course, you can also say "Ouch!" if you are the target of a mean comment.

REFLECT

At the end of each session, close with a circle and use the CircusSecret **reflect** for these questions: What went well? What could be better next time? Did I uphold each agreement? Take a moment to share. End on a positive note.

> **NOTE:** This circle process work was adapted from The Circle Way. Complete guidelines can be found at www.thecircleway.net/circle-way-guidelines.

Fig. 2 Dot voting.

Fig. 3 Ouch!

BUILDING AN ACT

Fig. 1 A flowing style.

Here's our "recipe" for putting tricks into a unified presentation. This method works for any circus skill (except clowning, which has different rules). It also works with non-circus skills (like fancy basketball dribbling, hacky sack, yo-yo, or RipStik).

Remember to use the Toolbox for Working Together and CircusSecrets on page 124 to help you stay focused and positive.

> **NOTE:** Here's the link to our companion online tutorial on building an act ABCs: www.DIYCircusLab.com/tutorials.

MATERIALS

* chosen circus prop(s)
* 5–10 white index cards (or cut paper)
* notebook paper and pencil
* friends

The Style and Hup*Hey!

The "style" is the "ta-da" at the end of a trick that signals the audience to applaud. Remember Bob and Norma from the pyramid unit?

At the very end of the whole act comes the "Hup*Hey!" The act captain shouts "HUP!" and then all the troupers clap once, and then they shout "HEY!" from the belly!

STEP 1: WRITE DOWN THE TRICKS

1. Choose your circus skill (juggling, stilts, etc.).

2. Write down a trick you can do on an index card.

3. Do this for each trick you (and your friends) can do.

4. Invent your own tricks and make up names for them. Write these down too.

STEP 2: PUT THE TRICKS IN ORDER

1. The most *basic* trick should be first.

2. The most *impressive* trick should be last.

3. Lay down the rest of the cards between the first and last tricks.

4. Copy the *act order* onto a piece of paper for rehearsals.

STEP 3: ADD MUSIC AND MOVEMENT

1. Find music that creates the right mood. (See "Music" on page 128.)

2. Add movements that enhance the act. For example, for a lyrical mood, create a graceful style *(Fig. 1)*, or create a flashy mood with a superhero style *(Fig. 2)*.

STEP 4: PRACTICE AND PERFORM

1. Choose the act captain who will run the rehearsals and keep things moving.

2. Practice the act until you've got it.

3. Style after tricks. Finish with a big Hup*Hey!

4. During practices, use the toolbox and CircusSecrets to create a positive experience.

5. Perform for your friends, family, the dog, or your goldfish Henry!

STEP 5: REFLECT

1. What went well?

2. It would be even better if...

GROUP ACTS

Your circus might need some acts with your whole troupe. Try making three for the beginning, middle, and end of your circus:

- **The "Chari Vari"** opens the show. It's a high-energy act where each trouper runs on, does a little stunt, and then zips off. It ends with everyone shouting Hup*Hey! You could show a sign with your circus's name.
- **Group juggling** is for the middle. Everyone juggles lots of stuff *(Fig. 3)*!
- **The pyramid act** is for the awesome grand finale. See Unit 4.

Once you have your acts, you'll link them together into your show.

Fig. 2 A flashy style.

Fig. 3 Practicing the group juggling act.

BUILDING A SHOW

MATERIALS

* colored index cards (or cut paper)
* notebook paper and pencil
* giant easel paper and a fat marker
* all the circus props, troupers, music, and costumes
* snare drum and cymbal (optional)

Music

Music is the invisible partner of your circus. It's almost impossible to imagine a circus without music, so choose it carefully. The music you select for each act should also shift the mood from one act to the next. Think twice about using songs with words because the audience's attention is split between watching you and listening to the lyrics. And if at all possible, have live music—it creates an entirely different experience than recorded tunes and is well worth the extra effort!

For circus music suggestions, see Resources on page 143.

NOTE: Here's the link to our companion online tutorial on building a Show ABCs: www.DIYCircusLab.com/tutorials.

Fig. 1 Post the show order.

It's good to have adult allies to help you get organized, stay safe, and keep track of things, but do as much as possible on your own. Use your agreements and toolbox to work together!

STEP 1: WRITE DOWN THE ACTS

Use colored cards for each type of skill (Fig. 1). For example:

partner acrobatics, pyramids	balance	spinning
clowning/ running gag	juggling	

STEP 2: PUT THE ACTS IN ORDER

1. If you have group acts, lay out cards for the Chari Vari (first act), the Group Juggling (middle), Pyramids (final act), and Running Gag (interspersed).

2. Insert the other acts into an order you like. The key is not having two cards in a row of the same color.

3. Copy the show order onto notebook paper and on giant paper. Post the giant paper on the wall for your troupe to refer to during the show (Fig. 2).

STEP 3: PRACTICE AND PERFORM

1. Choose a show captain to keep things moving and make final decisions.

2. Rehearse until the show feels ready. (Okay, it will never feel ready. Rehearse until it's showtime!)

3. Use the toolbox, your agreements, and the CircusSecrets to keep things positive.

4. Costumes: Wear the T-shirts you made, or whatever you like.

5. Sound effects: A drum roll on snare and a cymbal crash when the trick is done contributes to that circusy feeling. Can you borrow them?

6. Perform your circus (Fig. 3)!

STEP 4: REFLECT

1. What went well?

2. It would be even better if . . .

Yes, for sure there are a hundred more details to making a show—it would take another whole book to explain them all. What we've given you is a framework with lots of space for your own ideas. You'll find what works for you in the process of circus making—and don't worry, you're creative and thoughtful enough to work it out. Making a circus is WORK—but it is also—and most importantly—FUN. For sure.

Fig. 3 Showtime!

GROWING CIRCUS IN YOUR COMMUNITY

New England Center for Circus Arts (NECCA), Brattleboro, VT.
Credit: Jeff Lewis.

Done with this book? But not with circus! We hope you'll keep growing your circus skills—but you can also grow more circus around you. Let your community know that you love circus! You'll be amazed how many people want to learn about your skills.

Add your own ideas to this list—and happy circus making!

- Host a circus prop-making party. Make extras to donate to a local kids' program.
- Start a circus meet-up in a public park when the weather is nice.
- Create a circus practice group that helps you and your friends set and meet your circus goals.
- Start a juggling club at your school or place of worship.
- Clown at a senior center or daycare. (This could fulfill your community service requirement.)
- Do circus in a local parade: July 4, Memorial Day, Labor Day.
- Perform some circus in class plays, talent shows, fundraisers, dance recitals, or band concerts.
- Make visual art inspired by circus and display it at your local school, art center, or library.
- Take gymnastics, dance, or other circusy movement classes to add into your circus practice.
- Ask your teachers to integrate circus at school—history, science, arts, and math all have interesting and exciting circus applications! (Show them Appendix A in this book!)
- And of course, find some circus classes. Bring friends.

As Rick Davis said, you are capable of doing things that you never thought you could do before. You can go as far as your willpower, and your interest, and your motivation will take you.

So go forth and do circus! Because circus is for everyone. You're entirely perfect for sharing it!

Circus of Hope, Austin, TX. Credit: Ryan Taylor.

Wise Fool New Mexico, Santa Fe, NM. Credit: Gabriella Marks.

What about Insurance?

In the United States these days, people expect organized youth groups (even small-potatoes circus clubs) to have some kind of insurance.

Check out the Exploring program (www.exploring.org), an affiliate of the Boy Scouts of America. I insured my mom-and-pop summer camp with them for many years—the policy covered me, my coaches, the campers, and the buildings we used as "additionally insured." First, find a Boy Scout Council near you at www.exploring.org/contact-us. Then contact your local council and ask how to "sponsor a post or club" through the Exploring program for your recreational circus club. Exploring is a hands-on character and career education program for young people aged ten to twenty years old.

Otherwise, you might find coverage under your local school or community organization.

For serious, organized circus programs, there are insurance possibilities at www.americancircuseducators.org/insurance.

School for Acrobatics and New Circus Arts (SANCA), Seattle, WA. Credit: Erica Rubenstein.

CIRCUS AS A SERIOUS TOOL FOR LEARNING

When we look beyond circus's historical role as popular entertainment, we find that it can be a powerful educational tool providing rich opportunities for interdisciplinary, cross-curricular learning. Tap into the multifaceted circus industry to bring your curriculum to life. Here are some possibilities:

Business and marketing—Administration, box office, concessions, entrepreneurship, finance, media, merchandising, posters, profit and loss, programs, publicity releases, statistics, touring costs and logistics.

Community—Involve parent and elder volunteers, public performance for a cause, school community (all grades).

Cultural diversity—Study biographies of circus performers, circus as a multinational industry, world languages through circus, locate famous performers' homelands, study circus culture in different countries.

Evaluation—During the circus-making process, use journaling, photo/video documentation, reflection, self-assessment, examples of building the act, evidence of practice, creative expression.

History—Create a timeline of circus history from Roman circuses to Cirque du Soleil and beyond: hippodromes, Philip Astley (founder of modern circus), the Golden Age of circus,

P. T. Barnum, circus trains and the military industry, big tops vs. arenas, home-schooled circus children, contemporary vs. traditional circus, the state of contemporary circus today.

Interdisciplinarity—Teachers collaborate across arts, language, music, physical education, science.

Language development—Circus idioms and lingo (the origins of the term *jumbo*), circus-related acrostics, journaling, poetry, prose, tongue twisters. Create a circus dictionary. Discuss hyperbole on old circus posters. Be a reporter at your own show. Circus as depicted in fiction.

Medical—Injuries and injury prevention, hospital clowning (Big Apple Circus's "Clown Care"), circus-based occupational therapy.

Music—Composition for school circus, historical perspectives (American circus band Windjammers), playing in a school/community circus band.

Performing arts and production—Costumes, lighting, props, scene design, sound, stage management, roustabouts (crew). Examine how circus is portrayed in film and on stage. Attend and review a live circus performance.

Physical development—Balance, competence, endurance, eye-hand coordination, flexibility, eye-foot coordination, individual strengths, manual dexterity, physical literacy, physical skill assessments.

Science—Anatomy, axis, center of gravity, centrifugal/centripetal force, dynamic load, equilibrium, falling bodies, metabolism, nadir, static load, torque, vestibular system, zenith, why highwire walkers use long poles.

Shop class—Build all the DIY props in this book—and improve on them!

Social and emotional development—Use circus to teach CircusSecrets: self-awareness, self-management, social awareness, relationship skills, and responsible decision making. Circus also builds teamwork, trust, confidence, friendship, and persistence.

Visual arts—View circus through the art history lenses of Calder, Chagall, Degas, Gersch, Matisse, Picasso, Renoir, Rouault, Seurat, Toulouse-Lautrec. Build *Calder's Circus* sculptures. Paint a backdrop. Explore circus posters through time.

CIRCUSSECRETS AND SOCIAL AND EMOTIONAL LEARNING

The CircusSecrets were developed over hundreds of Circus Smirkus school residencies with thousands of children. Residency artist Rick Davis found that commonsense advice for learning circus skills also helped kids navigate personal and social situations. Teachers reported that their students continued to use CircusSecrets after the Smirkus residency ended.

In her doctoral work, Jackie aligned the CircusSecrets to five core competencies in Social and Emotional Learning (SEL): self-awareness, self-management, social awareness, relationship skills, and responsible decision making. These skill sets, identified by the Collaborative for Academic, Social, and Emotional Learning (CASEL), contribute to success in social roles and in life. A 2017 study showed that circus programs can impact youth SEL to equal or greater degree than other youth programs.

Self-awareness is the ability to recognize your emotions and assess your strengths and limitations. CircusSecrets: PAUSE (self-perception) and IMAGINE (growth mind-set, self-efficacy).

Self-management is the ability to set goals, manage expectations for achieving them, and delay gratification. CircusSecrets: TRY, TRY AGAIN, TRY A NEW WAY (self-motivation, discipline) and GO SLOW, STEP-BY-STEP (impulse control, stress management).

Social awareness is the ability to empathize with others, take the perspective of people who are different, and be respectful. CircusSecrets: WATCH, LISTEN (notice nonverbal and verbal cues for social norms).

Relationship skills foster communication, cooperation, and problem solving. CircusSecrets: GET HELP (communication), GIVE HELP (relationship building, teamwork).

Responsible decision making is the ability to make positive choices personally and in social situations, understand the consequences of actions, and consider the safety and well-being of yourself and others. CircusSecrets: STOP, THINK, AND CHOOSE (identify and analyze problems), REFLECT (evaluate).

For more information on social and emotional learning, go to www.casel.org.

CircusSecrets	CASEL Social and Emotional Core Competencies
Pause, Imagine	Self-awareness
Try, Try Again, Try a New Way; Go Slow, Step-by-Step	Self-management
Watch, Listen	Social awareness
Get Help, Give Help	Relationship skills
Stop, Think, and Choose; Reflect	Responsible decision making

APPENDIX B

THE ORIGINS OF YOUTH CIRCUS

As far as we know, the first youth circus was founded in 1929 by circus veteran Roy Coble. He offered a small family

The Great All-American Youth Circus, Redlands, CA.
Credit: Amber Wallick.

night circus at the YMCA in Redlands, California, that would bloom into the Great All-American Youth Circus, which is still going strong today.

Between 1929 and about 1960, youth circus programs sprouted up to promote positive youth development, including two collegiate circuses. In 1931, Clifford Horton brought his YMCA and gymnastics coaching experience to Illinois State University students where, with support from local trapeze artists, the Gamma Phi Circus was born. In 1947, Jack Haskin brought his experience in Gymkana (gymnastics entertainment) to Florida State University and started the Flying High Circus.

Meanwhile, in the Netherlands, Circus Elleboog was founded by Ida ter Haar in 1949 to keep kids off the streets after World War II. In the same year, Bill Rutland began the Sailor Circus as part of the Sarasota High School gymnastics curriculum in Florida. In Washington State in 1952, middle

school teacher Paul Pugh, who had connections to the YMCA, founded the Wenatchee Youth Circus. And in 1960 in Peru, Indiana, the Peru Amateur Circus was formed to revive the town's circus history and, to this day, 200 kids participate in its summer Circus City festivals.

Sailor Circus Academy, Sarasota, FL.
Credit: Sailor Circus Academy.

But around the 1950s and 1960s, television's popularity exploded and sent professional circuses into a tailspin. It wasn't until the 1970s that a new kind of circus emerged with different ideas. This "new circus" brought circus out of the big tops and into parks, church halls, schools, and the streets.

Where traditional circus featured trained animals, new circus included only the human kind. Where traditional circus families passed their secrets down the family line, new circus was available to ordinary folks like you and me—folks of all backgrounds and abilities. New circus was for *everyone*! Between 1971 and 1974, new circuses popped up in France (Le Cirque Bonjour), California (the Royal Lichtenstein Quarter-Ring Sidewalk Circus and the Pickle Family Circus), and Australia (New Circus, which became Circus Oz).

In 1974, a famous clown named Annie Fratellini opened a circus school in France—the first circus school in the West. One of her students, a lively Englishman named Reg Bolton, soon left to teach circus to a group of low-income children in a housing project in Scotland. Reg, who founded the Suitcase Circus in 1975, was among the first to include ordinary children and teens as *participants* in

Reg Bolton. Credit: Nic Ellis.

circus making. Until his death in 2006, Reg Bolton spread circus everywhere, especially to children in need, a practice we now call *social circus*.

SOCIAL CIRCUS

While some youth circus programs focus on recreation, *social circus* programs intentionally use circus as a means for personal growth and transformation. Social circus has a purpose: to lift up and empower participants who struggle with life's challenges, whether at home, in school, or on the streets. A major player in the social circus sector is *Cirque du Monde*, the social action arm of Canada's Cirque du Soleil, which supports partnerships in more than eighty communities across the globe. Jessica Hentoff of Circus Harmony writes, "Social circus is about helping young people to overcome not only gravity but labels and other limitations placed on them by society. It is about giving children the power to define themselves."

Social circus program in Abidjan, West Africa. Credit: Éric St-Pierre © 2001 Cirque du Soleil.

Social circus builds a sense of belonging among participants, then builds bridges between the circus group and the larger community. Through circus activities, participants learn to see the potential in themselves and each other, and learn to give back to their communities. In turn, communities learn to recognize these groups for their assets rather than their liabilities. In this way, circus-making becomes an agent for positive social change, and it's doing just that all around the world.

Afghan Mobile Mini Circus for Children in Afghanistan. Credit: Natsuyuki Imagawa.

APPENDIX C: YOUTH AND SOCIAL CIRCUS WORLDWIDE

YOUTH AND SOCIAL CIRCUS IN THE USA

(For our complete and current list, go to www.DIYCircusLab.com.)

1. Actors Gymnasium (Evanston, IL)
www.actorsgymnasium.org

2. Aloft Contemporary Circus Arts
(Chicago, IL)
www.aloftloft.com

3. Amazing Grace CIRCUS! (Nyack, NY)
www.amazinggracecircus.org

4. Arkansas Circus Arts (Little Rock, AR)
www.arkansascircusarts.com

5. ArtFarm (Middletown, CT)
www.art-farm.org

6. Berkcirque (Great Barrington, MA)
www.berkcirque.com

7. Bindlestiff Family Circus (NYC)
www.bindlestiff.org/education

8. Boulder Circus Center (Boulder, CO)
www.bouldercircuscenter.net

9. CircEsteem (Chicago, IL)
www.circesteem.org

10. Circus Academy of Tuscon
(Tuscon, AZ)
https://circusacademytucson.com

11. Circus Arts Institute (Atlanta, GA)
www.circusartsinstitute.com

12. Circus Center (San Francisco, CA)
www.circuscenter.org

13. Circus Culture (Ithaca, NY)
www.circusculture.org

14. Circus Juventas (St. Paul, MN)
www.circusjuventas.org

15. Circus Maine (Portland, ME)
www.circusmaine.org

16. Circus Mojo (Ludlow, KY)
www.circusmojo.com

17. Circus of Hope (Austin, TX)
www.circusofhope.org

18. Circus Place (Hillsborough, NJ)
www.thecircusplace.com

19. The Circus Project (Portland, OR)
www.thecircusproject.org

20. Circus Smirkus
(Greensboro, VT)
www.smirkus.org

21. Circus Up! (Roxbury, MA)
www.circusup.com

22. Circus Waldissima (Santa Rosa, CA)
www.circuswaldissima.com

23. Cirque du Jour (Orlando, FL)
www.cirquedujour.com

24. Dance & Circus Arts of Tampa Bay
(Clearwater, FL)
www.danceandcircusarts.com

25. Diamond Circus (Boston, MA)
www.diamondcircus.com

26. Esh Circus Arts (Somerville, MA)
www.eshcircusarts.com

27. Fern Street Circus (San Diego, CA)
www.fernstreetcircus.com

28. Fly Circus Space (New Orleans, LA)
www.flycircus.space

29. Flying Gravity Circus (Wilton, NH)
www.flyinggravitycircus.org

30. Flying High Circus (Tallahassee, FL)
www.circus.fsu.edu

31. Gamma Phi Circus (Normal, IL)
www.gammaphicircus.illinoisstate.edu

32. Great All-American Youth Circus
(Redlands, CA)
www.ycircus.org

33. Green Light Circus (Talkeetna, AK)
www.roustaboutcircus.com/
green-light-circus-alaska

34. H.I.C.C.U.P. Circus (Pahoa, HI)
www.hawaiispace.com/hiccup

35. Kinetic Circus Arts (Oakland, CA)
www.kineticartscenter.com

36. Lone Star Circus (Dallas, TX)
www.lonestarcircus.com

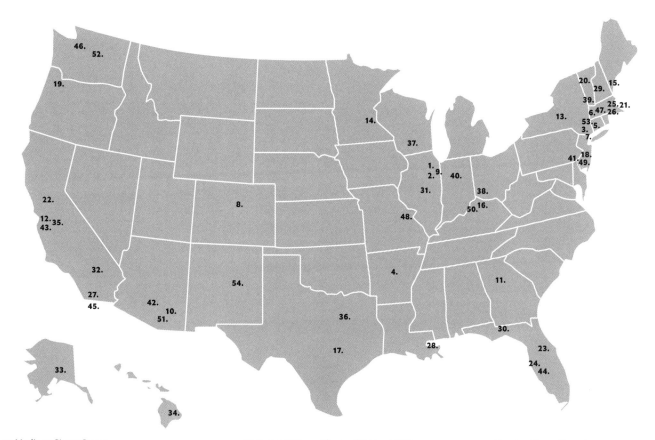

37. Madison Circus Space
(Madison, WI)
www.madisoncircusspace.com

38. My Nose Turns Red
(Cincinnati, OH)
www.mynoseturnsred.org

39. New England Center for Circus Arts
(Brattleboro, VT)
www.necenterforcircusarts.org

40. Peru Amateur Circus (Peru, IN)
www.peruamateurcircus.com

41. Philadelphia School of Circus Arts
(Philadelphia, PA)
www.phillycircus.com

42. Phoenix Youth Circus Arts
(Phoenix, AZ)
www.phxyouthcircus.org

43. Prescott Circus Theatre (Oakland, CA)
www.prescottcircus.org

44. Sailor Circus (Sarasota, FL)
http://circusarts.org/community-out-reach/sailor-circus

45. San Diego Circus Center
(San Diego, CA)
www.sandiegocircuscenter.org

46. School of Acrobatics & New Circus Arts
(Seattle, WA)
www.sancaseattle.org

47. SHOW Circus Studio
(Easthampton, MA)
www.showcircusstudio.com

48. St. Louis Arches/Circus Harmony
(St. Louis, MO)
www.circusharmony.org

49. Trenton Circus Squad
(Trenton, NJ)
www.trentoncircussquad.org

50. Turners Circus (Louisville, KY)
www.louisvilleturners.org

51. Tuscon Circus Arts
(Tuscon, AZ)
www.tusconcircusarts.com

52. Wenatchee Youth Circus
(Wenatchee, WA)
www.wenatcheeyouthcircus.com

53. Westchester Circus Arts
(Ardsley, NY)
www.westchestercircusarts.com

54. Wise Fool (Santa Fe, NM)
www.wisefoolnewmexico.org

INTERNATIONAL YOUTH AND SOCIAL CIRCUS

Africa: The African Circus Arts festival brings together young and professional artists from all over Africa to perform and take workshops. Ethiopia, Senegal, Kenya, Egypt, and more!
http://africancircusfestival.com

Asia: The Asian Social Circus Association, funded by Cirque du Soleil, helps support kids doing circus in Indonesia, Afghanistan, Cambodia, Vietnam, and many more.
http://www.socialcircus.org

Australasia: Youth circus is alive and well Down Under and in New Zealand. See for yourself at the Australian Circus and Physical Theater Association (ACAPTA):
http://acapta.org.au/acapta-directory/youth-circus-in-australia-and-new-zealand

Canada: Cirque du Soleil is world famous for its astounding circus performances. But it also devotes resources to its Cirque du Monde program, serving thousands of kids in social circus projects globally. This amazing map captures countless projects and organizations:
http://apps.cirquedusoleil.com/social-circus-map

Europe: CARAVAN's European Youth and Social Circus Network has 22 youth and social circus members.
www.caravancircusnetwork.eu

The European Youth Circus Organization has many member countries supporting kids' circus.
www.eyco.org

Older kids seeking higher education in circus arts can check out the European Federation of Professional Circus Schools (FEDEC): www.fedec.eu/en

Russia: In 1929, with the creation of the Moscow Circus School, Russia became the first country in the world to operate a state-run circus training facility.

South America: Social circus organizations in Peru, Chile, and Argentina received $3.6 million to help low-income kids get work in social circuses. Colombia and Brazil are set to follow. (The URL is too long, but Google "Multilateral Investment Fund" and "Cirque du Soleil.")

UK and Ireland: CircusWorks is the UK's youth circus network, creating festivals, conferences, and networking opportunities that strengthen the youth circus sector across England, Ireland, Northern Ireland, Scotland, and Wales.
www.circusworks.org.

For our complete list of worldwide youth and social circuses, go to www.DIYCircusLab.com.

Red Nose Foundation, Indonesia. Credit: Red Nose Foundation.

Flipside Circus, Australia. Credit: Flipside Circus.

Five Ring Circus, United Kingdom. Credit: Helen Averley.

Red Nose Foundation, Indonesia. Credit: Red Nose Foundation.

RESOURCES

UNIT 1: SPINNING AND FLOWING

HOW TO:

There are zillions of online tutorials for these skills. To get you started:

Diabolo tutorials: www.diabolotutorials.com

Hoop tutorials with Deanne Love (who inspired the hoop lessons in this book): www.hooplovers.tv

Juggling stick tutorials with Laura Bosken: www.youtube.com/watch?v=fDQR-SHuSHA

Poi tutorials with Nick Woolsey (who inspired the poi lessons in this book): www.playpoi.com/learn

SHOPPING:

www.firetoys.com
www.higginsbrothers.com
www.homeofpoi.com
www.renegadejuggling.com
www.superhooper.org

FURTHER STUDY:

Diabolo: History and background of Chinese yo-yo http://hua.umf.maine.edu/China/ModernBeijing/pages/286_ChineseYoyo.html

Diabolo: Origins of the modern diabolo www.juggle.org/c-b-fry-gustave-philippart-and-the-origins-of-modern-diabolo

Flow Arts: https://flowartsinstitute.com/about-us/what-is-flow-arts

Hoop Dance History: https://indiancountrymedianetwork.com/news/history-of-the-modern-hoop-dance

Hula hoop history: www.hooping.org/hula-hoop-history

Juggling sticks: A short history of devilstick www.juggle.org/a-short-history-of-devilstick

Poi history and culture: www.homeofpoi.com/us/lessons/teach/History-Culture/Poi-History

Poi: Maori origins of poi: www.themaori.com/maori-art/poi

UNIT 2: JUGGLING

HOW TO:

There's a gazillion juggling tutorials online. To get you started:

Juggling for beginners: www.juggling-for-beginners.com

SHOPPING:

www.dube.com

www.henrys-online.de/en

www.higginsbrothers.com

www.renegadejuggling.com

www.toddsmith.com

FURTHER STUDY:

Dancey, C. (1994). *The encyclopaedia of ball juggling*. Bath, England: Butterfingers.

Finnigan, D. (1991). *The complete juggler: All the steps from beginner to professional (3rd ed.)*. Jugglebug.

eJuggle: The official online publication of the International Jugglers' Association. www.juggle.org/ejuggle

Juggling—its history and greatest performers www.juggling.org/books/alvarez/part1.html

Ten female juggling stars of the past: www.juggle.org/10-female-juggling-stars-of-the-past

International Jugglers' Association www.juggle.org

Museum of Juggling History http://historicaljugglingprops.com

UNIT 3: BALANCE

HOW TO:

Rola bola: Beginner tips from Chris Silcox www.youtube.com/watch?v=QT3iOsiAQOM

Rola bola: Awesomely inspiring act from the 2010 Circus Smirkus Big Top Tour: www.youtube.com/watch?v=gfKgBTRK0KQ

Stilt Dancing: Inspiringly cool showcase by the Prescott Circus Theatre, 2013: www.youtube.com/watch?v=Y-556VKXzvg

Tightwire: More inspiration from the 2012 Circus Smirkus Big Top Tour: www.youtube.com/watch?v=6dC-XWx--20

SHOPPING:

www.firetoys.com

www.pegstilts.com

www.stiltfactory.com

www.unicycle.com

FURTHER STUDY:

McCredie, S. (2007). *Balance: In search of the lost sense*. New York: Little, Brown and Company

Rola bola: Bongo board history and evolution www.vewdo.com/Bongo-Board-Facts--Bongo-Board-History-Evolution_ep_85-1.html

Stilts: The magical world of international stilt-walkers. www.huffingtonpost.com/2014/08/11/laura-anderson-barbata_n_5659828.html

Tightrope: An Abridged History of Funambulists www.atlasobscura.com/articles/an-abridged-history-of-funambulists

Tightrope: The Blondin Memorial Trust: Funambulus www.blondinmemorialtrust.com/funambulus

UNIT 4: ACROBALANCE & PYRAMIDS

HOW TO:

Find a circus program near you! See Appendix C on
pages 136–138.

SHOPPING:

Mats: www.resilite.com/store/gymnastics/c-folding-mats,
www.matsmatsmats.com/gymnastics/mats/folding-
mat-is.html

FURTHER STUDY:

Blume, M. (2013). *Acrobatics for children and teenagers.*
Meyer & Meyer Sport (UK), Ltd.

Fodero, J. & Furblur, E. (1989). *Creating gymnastic pyramids
and balances.* Chicago: Leisure Press.

UNIT 5: CLOWNING

HOW TO:

Circus Smirkus Summer Camp
www.smirkus.org/smirkus-camp

Mooseburger Clown Camp (for adults, but look what's
offered!) www.mooseburger.com/moosecamp

Nose-to-Nose clowning workshops (teens or older)
www.nosetonose.info

SHOPPING:

www.clownantics.com
www.clownsupplies.com
www.firetoys.com (for Nils Poll juggling hats)

FURTHER STUDY:

Ballantine, B. (1982). *Clown alley.* Boston: Little, Brown
and Company.

Fife, B. et al. (1988). *Creative clowning.* Piccadilly Books.

Hugill, B. (1980). *Bring on the clowns.* Seacaucus, NJ:
Chartwell Books, Inc.

Pipkin, T. (1989). *Be a clown!* New York: Workman Publishing.

Schechter, J. (2001). *The Pickle Clowns: New American
circus comedy.* Southern Illinois University.

Towsen, J. H. (1976). *Clowns.* New York: E.P. Dutton.

"The Father of Pediatric Clown Care"
https://priceonomics.com/how-a-clown-brought-humor-
to-childrens-hospitals

Christian Clowning/Clown Ministry
http://worldclown.com/clown-ministry

Clowns International!
www.clownsinternational.com

Clowns Without Borders
www.clownswithoutborders.org

International Clown Hall of Fame & Research Center
www.theclownmuseum.com

Therapeutic Clowns International
www.therapeuticclownsinternational.com

World Clown Association www.worldclown.com

The Red Trouser Show: Longest hat toss ever? Slow motion!
https://youtu.be/HQHVV94L7Yw

Medical clowns: Humorology Atlanta, HA! (Children's Healthcare of Atlanta) www.humorologyatlanta.org

Medical clowns: Laughter League (a.k.a. Funnyatrics Clown Program), Children's Hospital, Dallas , TX www.childrens.com/patient-resources/visitor-patient-guide/activities-for-kids/funnyatrics-clown-program, www.laughterleague.org/blog

ONLINE RESOURCES FOR CIRCUS, YOUTH CIRCUS, AND SOCIAL CIRCUS

American Youth Circus Organization (AYCO) www.americanyouthcircus.org

Asian Social Circus Association www.socialcircus.org

Australian Circus & Physical Theatre Association (ACAPTA) www.acapta.org.au

CARAVAN Circus Network (Europe) www.caravancircusnetwork.eu

Circopedia www.circopedia.org

Circus 4 Youth www.circus4youth.org

Circus Federation www.circusfederation.org

Circus Historical Society www.circushistory.org

Circus in America: 1793-1940. www.circusinamerica.org

CircusWorks (UK and Ireland) www.circusworks.org

Effective Circus Project #1: *Well-being effects from social circus.* www.uta.fi/cmt/index/wellbeing-effects-from-social-circus.pdf

Effective Circus Project #2: *Studying social circus: Openings and perspectives.* www.uta.fi/cmt/index/Studying_Social_Circus.pdf

European Youth Circus Organization (EYCO) www.eyco.org

HUP Squad Youth Action Team Blog www.circusismylife.wordpress.com

Reg Bolton, articles and dissertation www.regbolton.org

Spectacle Magazine: An online journal of the circus arts. www.spectaclemagazine.com

CIRCUS MUSIC

Music for Youth Circus: *Rocking the Planets* by Leslie Vogel. www.store.cdbaby.com/cd/leslievogel3

Windjammers Unlimited, Inc.: A circus music historical society dedicated to the preservation of traditional circus music. www.circusmusic.org

PRINT

Albrecht, E. (2006). *The contemporary circus: Art of the spectacular*. Lanham, MD.: Scarecrow Press.

Bolton, R. (1982). *Circus in a suitcase*. Rowayton, CT: New Plays Incorporated.

Bolton, R. (1999). Circus as education. *Australasian Drama Studies, 35, 9.* www.regbolton.org/articles

Burgess, H., & Finelli, J. (1976). *Circus techniques: Juggling, equilibristics, vaulting*. New York: Thomas Y. Crowell Company.

Davis, R. (1994). *Totally useless skills*. Pages Publishing Group.

Hentoff, J. (2015, Spring). Social circus: A definition. *The Magazine of the American Circus Educators Association, 2* (4), 14–21. https://view.joomag.com/american-circus-educators-magazine-summer-2015-issue-2-vol-4/0571431001493174072

Jando, D., & Granfield, L. (2008). *The circus: 1870–1950.* N. Daniel (Ed.). Hong Kong: Taschen.

Levinson, C. (2015). *Watch out for flying kids! How two circuses, two countries, and nine kids confront conflict and build community.* Atlanta: Peachtree Publishers.

McMullen, R.D., and McNulty, K. (1985). *Circus in art: Illustrated talks on collections of the circus in art. Wiggin Gallery, Boston Public Library* on May 3, 1974. Boston Public Library.

Mermin, R. (1997). *Circus Smirkus: A true story of high adventure and low comedy.* Troll Press.

Roalf, P. (1993). *Looking at paintings: Circus.* New York: Hyperion Books for Children.

Sugarman, R. (2001). *Circus for Everyone: Circus Learning Around the World.* Shaftsbury, Vermont: Mountainside Press.

Wall, D. (2013). *The ordinary acrobat: A journey into the wondrous world of the circus, past and present.* New York: Alfred A. Knopf.

Wiley, J. (1974). *Basic circus skills.* Harrisburg, PA: Stackpole Books.

Woodhead, P. (2002). Report to the Winston Churchill Memorial Trust on in-school circus programs in the USA and UK. www.churchilltrust.com.au/fellows/detail/2651/Paul+WOODHEAD

ACADEMIC RESOURCES

Bolton, R. (2004). Why circus works: How the values and structures of circus make it a significant developmental experience for young people. *Unpublished doctoral dissertation.* Perth, Australia: Murdoch University. www.regbolton.org/why-circus-works-reg-bolton

Cohen, A. (2012). Cultivating contemporary circus culture: Investigating the factors that have limited the growth of circus as an art form in the United States. *Unpublished master's thesis.* New York: New York University.

Davis, J.L. (2011). Toward best practices in youth worker training for developmental circus arts programs. www.americancircuseducators.org/wp-content/uploads/2015/07/Core-Competencies-and-Best-Practices.pdf

Kiez, T. K. (2015). The impact of circus arts instruction on the physical literacy of children in grades 4 and 5. *Unpublished master's thesis.* Winnipeg: University of Manitoba. https://mspace.lib.umanitoba.ca/handle/1993/30711

McCutcheon, S. (2003). Negotiating identity through risk: A community circus model for evoking change and empowering youth. *Unpublished master's thesis.* Victoria, Australia: La Trobe University.

Ott, D. (2005). A phenomenology of youth circus training at Fern Street. *Unpublished doctoral dissertation.* Tempe, Arizona: Arizona State University.

Rappaport, S. (2014, August). Circus arts and occupational therapy: Gaining great performance. Tufts University conference poster. http://circusforsurvivors.com/wp-content/uploads/2015/01/allcircus_FINAL.pdf

Seymour, K. D. (2012). How circus training can enhance the well-being of autistic children and their families. *Unpublished master's thesis.* Griffith University. http://acapta.org.au/wp-content/uploads/2014/04/K.Seymourhonoursthesis.autismcircus.pdf

ABOUT THE CIRCUS LAB KIDS

Hi, I'm Ailiea. I'm twelve and I started circus at age five. Favorite skills: stilts, rola bola, and poi. I like vegetables!

Hi, I'm Cyan. I'm eleven and I started circus at age five. Favorite skills: doing flips and diabolo. My least favorite vegetable is eggplant.

Hi, I'm Ellie! I'm twenty-two and I started circus before I can remember. Favorite skills: clowning, handbalancing, and juggling. My least favorite vegetable is a bland tomato.

Hi, I'm Evalina. I'm seven and I started circus at age one! Favorite skills: pole, mini-tramp, and aerial square. My least favorite vegetable is mushrooms.

Hi, I'm Gigi. I'm nine and I started circus at birth. Favorite skills: aerials and animal training (with my dog, goats, and mini horse), and helping my mom make shows. Eggplant? YUK!

Hi, I'm Harrison. I'm fifteen and I started circus at age ten. Favorite skills: ball juggling, club juggling, and club passing. Vegetables are all good!

Hi, I'm Henry. I'm fourteen years old and I started circus at age eight. Favorite skills: unicycling, juggling, clown, and mime. Broccoli tastes bittery!

Hi, I'm Joshua. I'm sixteen and I started circus at age six. Favorite skills: tumbling and juggling. I don't like tomatoes and peas.

Hi, I'm Quin. I'm ten and I started circus at age four. Favorite skill: unicycling. My least favorite vegetable is Brussels sprouts.

Hi, I'm Shira. I'm fifteen and I started circus at age ten. Favorite skills: tightwire and pyramids. My least favorite vegetables are eggplant and avocados.

Hi, I'm Yasmin. I'm fifteen and I started circus at age seven. Favorite skills: juggling and unicycling. I don't like peas because they pop in your mouth.

Hi, I'm Zeb. I'm fourteen and I started circus when I was zero. I'm interested in circus lighting. My least favorite vegetable is okra.

ABOUT THE TEAM (AND SPOTTERS!)

Sara Morgan Greene (left) and her daughter Gigi have their own big top tent and run the Granite State Circus (www.granitestatecircus.com).

Serenity Smith Forchion (right) is a cofounder of the New England Center for Circus Arts (www.necenterforcircusarts.org). Sara and Serenity believe that traditional and contemporary circus arts empower students, invigorate communities, and enrich people's lives.

PHOTOGRAPHER, VIDEOGRAPHER, AND MAKERSPACE DIRECTOR

Scot Langdon began his photography career in the news industry, covering politics, metro news, and sports. He is a long-time fan of school and community circus performances. Scot enjoys working with individuals, non-profit organizations, and publications that communicate stories through his photographs. His passion is capturing his subjects' personalities in their natural surroundings. www.longhillphoto.com.

Steven E. Opre By day, Steve teaches STEM and pre-engineering concepts to middle school students; by night, he teaches statistics and technical mathematics at Nashua Community College. He's a founding member and director of the Amherst (NH) Makerspace where paying members use a public school industrial arts center as a community workshop. www.sau39.org/domain/492

Joseph Laszlo began filming town meetings when he was fifteen and videotaped his first school circus in 2011. He likes mime and knows how to juggle. Joseph is a Communications major with a film/video concentration and enjoys freelance videography. www.josephlaszlo.com

ABOUT THE AUTHOR

Jackie Leigh Davis has been teaching circus to children and teens since 1995. She's a founding member of the American Youth Circus Organization and established the middle school Hilltop Circus program at Pine Hill Waldorf School, the Flying Gravity Circus (a teen troupe), and the Silver Lining Circus Camp. She is an award-winning speaker and has presented internationally about how circus arts contribute to positive youth development.

In 2007, Jackie was named Middle School PE Teacher of the Year by the New Hampshire Association for Health, Physical Education, Recreation, and Dance. She is a graduate of the Spacial Dynamics Institute where she also served as adjunct faculty in circus arts education.

Jackie holds a master's degree in human development and psychology from the Harvard Graduate School of Education, and she completed two years of doctoral study at the University of British Columbia, where she studied the effects of circus arts on youth development. Jackie is now writing circus books for children and teens, including picture, chapter, and how-to books, as well as young adult fiction.

Prior to her teaching and writing careers, Jackie was a professional mime who studied with Marcel Marceau, entertained at Walt Disney World's Epcot Center, and performed countless shows with her husband, Rick. She resides in New Hampshire. Her adult daughters, Erin and Ellie, have grown and flown.

ABOUT CIRCUS SMIRKUS

Credit: Circus Smirkus.

Circus Smirkus is an award-winning international youth circus founded by Rob Mermin in Greensboro, Vermont, in 1987 to promote the skills, culture, and traditions of the traveling circus and to inspire youth to engage in life-changing adventures in the circus arts. Kids who got their start in the circus from an early age with Smirkus have gone on to perform with companies including Ringling Bros. and Barnum & Bailey Circus, Cirque du Soleil, and Big Apple Circus. About one in five of all Smirkos in the Big Top Tour have pursued a professional career in the circus.

Since our first shows thirty years ago, Circus Smirkus has grown to include the Big Top Tour, Smirkus Camp, and Ringmaster Residencies, engaging tens of thousands of youth and adults each year as performers, audience members, campers, and circus dreamers. The Big Top Tour is the only American youth circus to travel "under canvas," putting on a full-season tour under its own big top, a 750-seat, one-ring, European-style tent. Our thirty troupers range in age from ten to eighteen and are completely immersed in life on the road and truly learn what it is to be "circus people." In the summer months, Smirkus runs one- and two-week residential circus camps, from Smirkling Camp for the youngest children to advanced sessions for aspiring performers up to age eighteen. During the school year, Smirkus offers its artist-in-residency program to schools in Vermont and around New England, bringing circus skills and the Smirkus values of inclusion, self-worth, dedication, and possibility to reach your dreams into the classroom.

To learn more about Circus Smirkus and how you can follow your dream of running away with the circus, please visit us at www.smirkus.org.

ACKNOWLEDGMENTS

I'm exceedingly grateful to these amazing people!
A huge circus THANK YOU to:

Ed LeClair, who has been my fairy godfather since 2014; and Rob Mermin, who founded Circus Smirkus through which *so much* has happened.

The incredibly gifted (and patient) DIY Circus Lab Kids: Ailiea, Cyan, Evalina, Gigi, Harrison, Henry, Josh, Quin, Shira, Yasmin, and Zeb; and Ellie for multi-tasking as Lab Kid, chauffeur, and Running Gag Consultant.

The AYCO/ACE community, particularly Jesse Alford, Amy Cohen, Jessica Hentoff, Ted Lawrence, Carlo Pellegrini, and Bev Sobelman. Thanks to my fellow AYCONs for contributing your photos! Special thanks to Sara Morgan Greene for her expertise in rigging, knots, and technical drawing—also for spotting along with Serenity Smith Forchion (thanks for your children, too)!

The amazing circademic team that compiled the list of worldwide youth and social circus: Brianna Marie Wegrzyn, Audrey Djunaedi, and Lloyd D. Scharneck, Jr. with Lynn Carroll, Ulla Hokkanen, Pip Scott, and Daniel Simu.

The Circademics Facebook community for abundant advice, especially Matt Gupwell of *Teach Circus in Schools* in the UK, Lund Lundson (devil stick historian), Jaime Bouvier, and Shay Erlich (hoop advice).

Ringling Brothers Clown Alley members, particularly Steve Russell and Steven Michael Harris, for Running Gag advice.

International Jugglers' Association members Lukas Reichenbach and David Cain for help finding vintage images.

The geeks at Amherst Makerspace who problem-solved the homemade diabolo: Marcel Chabot and especially Joe Gaudreau, who thought of using lug nuts (Eureka!).

Nancy Rosenfeld and my old friend David Tabatsky who helped me with my contract.

The team at Quarry Books for mentoring me through this process: Cara Connors, Marissa Giambrone, Karen Levy, Lara Neel, and Jonathan Simcosky.

Jamie Ferrier and the Unitarian Universalist Congregation of Milford for scheduling and hosting our photo shoots.

My steadfast Three Musketeers—Scot Langdon, Joseph Laszlo, and Steve Opre—who made this project possible! And to Kim Stratton at Ambient Design and Nina Eppes, Matt Frost, David Graham for saving the day.

Jen Agans, Jon Roitman, and Jacob Skeffington for two decades of circus education conversation (especially at 3 a.m.) and for co-coining *Achievable Basic Competency* in our discussions of circus literacy.

Leslie Vogel, whose circus music is the sound track of my life; the Hilltop Circus at Pine Hill Waldorf School where this whole adventure began; and the Flying Gravity Circus where this whole adventure continues.

And my sistah, Barbara Thorngren, for the Circle Way information and… for being there. We have walked together through the darkest night, and look—the sun is rising!

INDEX